†HE Last Hour

PROPHECY, WORLD VIEWS & UFO's

Jim Simmons

Fairway Press, Lima, Ohio

THE LAST HOUR: PROPHECY, WORLD VIEWS & UFO'S
FIRST EDITION
Copyright © 2001 by Jim Simmons

All rights reserved. No portion of this book may be reproduced or utilized in any form or by any means, electronic or mechanical including photocopying, without permission in writing from the publisher. Inquiries should be addressed to: Fairway Press, 517 South Main Street, P.O. Box 4503, Lima, Ohio 45802-4503. www.fairwaypress.com or www.csspub.com.

Library of Congress Control Number: 2001 131432

Quotations from the New American Standard Bible (NASB), published by the Lockman Foundation © 1960, 1962, 1963, 1968, 1971, are used by permission.
Quotations from the New International Version of the Bible (NIV), published by the Zondervan Corporation, copyright © 1978 by the New York International Bible Society. Used by permission.
Quotations marked KJV are from the Authorized or King James Version of the Bible.
Quotations from New King James Version of the Bible (NKJV), copyright © 1979, 1980, 1982, by Thomas Nelson, Inc. Used by permission.
Quotations from *Mere Christianity*, by C. S. Lewis, published by Simon & Schuster, copyright © 1943, 1945, 1952 by Macmillan Publishing Company, a division of Macmillan Inc., copyright © renewed by Arthur Owen Barfield, 1980. Used by permission of Harper Collins Ltd.
Chart from *Counseling and the Nature of Man*, by Frank Minirth, M.D., Paul Meier, M.D., published by Baker Book House, Grand Rapids, Michigan 49506, copyright © 1982. Used by permission.

ISBN 0-7880-1673-3   PRINTED IN U.S.A.

Dedication and Acknowledgment

For my mother, Christine Simmons, who was a diligent student and teacher of God's Word. May her legacy live on.

For my wife, Joanne Shipley Simmons, who not only supported and encouraged me as I wrote, but who also assisted me with suggestions and editorial help. Words cannot adequately express my appreciation. She has been a tremendous blessing to me as my wife, friend and helper.

I would also like to acknowledge and thank Wayne Francis, my friend and brother in Christ, for the charts and diagrams used in this book. His skill and ability in this area were invaluable.

My thanks also to my friend and sister in Christ, Judy Jones Fairchild, for her encouragement, suggestions and proof reading.

My thanks to many others who have assisted and encouraged me in this project.

It is my prayer that God's word will continue to be spread through our children and that Jesus Christ will be glorified in the heart of the reader. May God's promise be realized. "So shall My word be which goes forth from My mouth; it shall not return to Me empty, without accomplishing what I desire, and without succeeding in the matter for which I sent it" (Isaiah 55:11 NASB).

CONTENTS

INTRODUCTION

LIST OF CHAPTERS, WITH SUBTITLES   6

LIST OF CHAPTERS, WITHOUT SUBTITLES
    Chapter 1: Will the Real Prophet Stand Up?   15
    Chapter 2: Generation X - the Last Generation?   39
    Chapter 3: World Views from a Human and
                    Divine Perspective   61
    Chapter 4: Signs of the Times   87
    Chapter 5: New Age Apostasy   107
    Chapter 6: UFO's! Extraterrestrials! Millions Missing!   127
    Chapter 7: Apocalypse / Last Days   159

LIST OF CHARTS
    Chart 1   Daniel's 70 Weeks   32
    Chart 2   Times of the Gentiles   42
    Chart 3   Killer Earthquakes   49
    Chart 4   Changing World View - Philosophy   65
    Chart 5   Four Types of Therapy   74-75
    Chart 6   Growth of Knowledge   89
    Chart 7   Interrelationships Between Seal, Trumpet
                  and Bowl Judgments   190

APPENDIX A
    For the Reader's Consideration   209

APPENDIX B
    List of Tribulation Judgments (Seals, Trumpets,
         and Bowls)   213

FOOTNOTES   217

BIBLIOGRAPHY   229

LIST OF CHAPTERS, WITH SUBTITLES

CHAPTER ONE
WILL THE REAL PROPHET STAND UP?

Modern Day Beliefs about the Future	15
Why Study Prophecy?	16
Biblical Reliability	17
Missing Day	18
Prophet or Fraud?	20
Old Testament Prophecies	22
Alexander the Great: an Important Figure in Prophetic History	23
Greek: a Providential Language	25
Judgment on Israel	26
Fulfillment of the Judgment of Israel	28
Daniel's 70 Weeks: a Phenomenal Prophecy	29
Mystery of the Church Age	33
Jesus Christ - the Fulfillment of the Old Testament Prophets	34
Chance Fulfillment	35
Brief Summary of the Old Testament Prophecies Fulfilled in Christ	36

CHAPTER TWO
GENERATION X - THE LAST GENERATION

Miraculous Rebirth of a Nation	39
Four World Empires	40
Israel, God's Time Piece	43
Parable of the Fig Tree	44
Signs of the End Times	45
Birth Pangs	47
Earthquakes	48
Climate Changes	50
Wars and Rumors of Wars	51

Increase in Immorality and Violence	54
Persecution of Christians	55
Future Predictions from a Human Perspective	56

CHAPTER THREE
WORLD VIEWS FROM A HUMAN AND DIVINE PERSPECTIVE

Mind Benders	61
Immanuel Kant	62
Georg Hegel	62
Soren Kierkegaard	63
Charles Darwin	63
Changing World View	64
Psychology: a Brief Historical Review	64
Psychoanalysis	64
Analytical Psychology	66
Existential Analysis	67
Humanistic Psychology: Human Potential Movement	67
Rogerian Therapy	68
Mysticotranscendent Approach	68
Behavioral Therapies	69
Changing World View (Psychology)	69
Psychotherapy Pitfalls	71
Man's Nature: an Understanding of the Problem	72
Two Kingdoms / Two Foundations	76
Where Is Your Thermometer?	79
Contrasting World Views / Belief Systems	81
Faith and Reason	82

Chapter Four
SIGNS OF THE TIMES

Knowledge Explosion	87
Real Generation Gap	88
Internet - Knowledge Communication Explosion	90
Babel Revisited	91
The Quickening	92
Environmental Manipulation - Who Is in Control?	94
One World Culture	95
Control the Media / Control the World	96
Visibility of the Media Industry	97
Digital Media Deception	97
Reporting the News or Creating the News?	98
One World / Global Control	100
Environmental Concerns or a Hidden Agenda?	101
The Money Connection	102
Global Unity	104

Chapter Five
NEW AGE APOSTASY

New Age or Ancient Religion in Disguise?	107
New Age Cloaks Occult	109
Do All Roads Lead to Rome?	110
The Gospel According to the New Age	112
Prophecy According to the New Age	115
Mystery Babylon, the Harlot	117
One World Government, One World Religion, and One Trigger	122
Coincidence or Divine Providence?	123

CHAPTER SIX
UFO'S! EXTRATERRESTRIALS! MILLIONS MISSING!

Do UFO's Really Exist?	127
The Mexico Flap	128
The Israel Flap	129
Apollo 11 Sightings	130
Roswell Incident	131
The UFO World View	132
ET's and the New Age Prophets	133
UFO's and ET's, "the World's Reality"	134
Ancient Visitors or Astronauts?	136
Men and "gods"	137
Where Do UFO's and Aliens Come From?	139
Science in the New Age - How Many Dimensions?	140
New Physics: Quantum What?	142
Aliens! Who Are They? What Are They Saying?	146
The UFO / Rapture Connection	148
The New Age Rapture	151

CHAPTER SEVEN
APOCALYPSE / LAST DAYS

Rapture Shock	159
Pentecost Reversal	160
Overview of the Ages	162
Times of the Gentiles - Began in 606 B.C.	
with Captivity of Judah	162
Israel's Clock - Daniel's 70 Weeks Prophecy	163
Prophetic Clocks	164
Time Gap	165
Right at the Door	166
The Longest 7 Years in History: the Tribulation Period	168
Character Lineup	168
Antichrist	168

"Out of the Sea"	169
Man of Sin	169
False Prophet: Looks like a Lamb,	
Talks like a Dragon	170
"Out of the Earth"	170
The Man Behind the Man	171
Miracles and Images	171
The Good Guys: the Two Witnesses	173
A Multitude of Jewish Evangelists: Sealing of	
144,000 Jews for Jesus	175
On the Starting Block	175
One White Horse / One "Bad News" Rider	176
The Ultimate Politician	177
A Temple Rebuilt	178
The Other Side of the Curtain: a Supernatural War	179
The UFO / ET Connection	180
A Red Horse Warrior	183
Broken Covenant	183
The Russian Confederacy Invasion	183
The Balance of Power: God's Strategy	185
The Vacuum: a Power Shift	186
Russian Update	186
War, Famine, Poverty	187
The Black Horse: Starvation and Poverty	188
The Pale Horse: Deadly Rider	188
Four Horsemen: An Overview of the Tribulation Period	189
Blood of the Martyrs: Fifth Seal	189
Convulsions of Planet Earth: Sixth Seal	191
Ecological Horrors: Seventh Seal	
Trumpet Judgements	191
The Demonic Trumpets: the Final Trumpets	194
The Antichrist Would like to See Your I.D.	195
The Demonic Asian Invasion	196
The Final Stretch: God's Wrath on Earth	
Bowl Judgements	198

First Bowl: Malignant Sores	198
Second Bowl: Sea Turns to Blood /	
All Sea Creatures Die	198
Third Bowl: Rivers and Springs Turn to Blood	199
Fourth Bowl: Men Scorched with Heat	199
Fifth Bowl: Darkness	200
Sixth Bowl: Euphrates River Dries up	200
Seventh Bowl: "It Is Done"	
Lightning, Thunder, Earthquake, Hail	201
Antichrist and False Prophet: an Alien Connection?	202
Armageddon: the Final Conflict	203
Heaven's Invasion	203
The Final Act	205

INTRODUCTION

As we move further into the third millennium, there is a sense of anticipation in the air. Many books have been published concerning prophecy and the return of Jesus Christ.

People who are oriented toward a New Age philosophy and who do not believe in the events prophesied in the Bible, also have a sense that something cataclysmic is about to occur. Part of that anticipation is certainly because of the movement into the third millennium. There was also some fear concerning Y2K (Year 2000) and the condition of our country and the world. From a popular secular viewpoint, these are valid concerns about the future of the human race.

This book is not intended to be a comprehensive book on prophecy. Rather, it is a snapshot of prophecy as it relates to our time in light of what the Bible says regarding current events, technology, the New Age movement, the UFO movement, and the changing world view. It simply gives an orientation of Biblical prophecy from several perspectives in our current time frame.

The purpose of this book is to sensitize people toward the supernatural and its reality. Hopefully, it will help the reader view reality from a slightly different perspective. We cannot see the supernatural through our five senses because it is veiled from us. In the book of Corinthians Paul says, "For now we see in a mirror dimly but then face to face; now I know in part, but then I shall know fully just as I also have been fully known" (I Corinthians 13:12 NASB).

The reader cannot go beyond seeing in that "mirror dimly" but my prayer is to be available as one of God's instruments in bringing the reader to the reality of the mirror and the existence of a personal God operating behind the mirror. Another purpose of this book is to help the reader discern the difference between the validity and content of God's Word (reality) and what the world offers (delusion).

My hope and prayer is that after reading this book the reader will gain a greater awareness of God's reality and a new or renewed relationship with Jesus Christ.

With great anticipation, we look forward to meeting Him and "knowing fully as I [we] have been fully known."

-ONE -

WILL THE REAL PROPHET STAND UP?

"Where there is no vision, the people perish. . . ."
Proverbs 29:18 KJV

Throughout the history of mankind, people have searched for ways to discover what the future holds. This chapter covers future events by unlocking Biblical prophecy.

This chapter will help the reader to understand Bible prophecy. It will also show reasons why we can trust the Biblical prophets and how to test their reliability and authority.

MODERN DAY BELIEFS ABOUT THE FUTURE

The future fascinates us. What does the future hold? What does God say about the future? What does the Bible say about the future?

With the new millennium, people have various opinions about what the future holds. In spite of terrorist activities and the threat of biological and/or chemical weapons, Americans on the whole remain positive, as shown in the following newspaper article.

> Still, four out of five people in a poll by the Pew Research Center for the People and the Press say they are hopeful about life in the new millennium. That hopeful outlook is fueled by their faith in science and technology, modern medicine and higher education.

> Previous polls also have shown American optimism is based largely on the roaring economy. "I think optimistically about the future because I don't want to think negatively," said Janice Royce of Anchorage, Alaska . . . . "The economy is great. Politics will always be politics, but I like the direction the country is going in."[1]

Other statistics give a more pessimistic outlook. Approximately two out of three people expect a major terrorist attack on this country through biological or chemical warfare. They also fear a worldwide threat through an energy crisis and environmental problems.[2]

The Pew Research Center for the People and the Press conducted a poll about expectations beyond the year 2000. Approximately 84% (as an average) of Americans believe that the following three major areas will play a major role in improving life: medical advances 85%; Science and technology 89%; and Schools and Universities 79%. These were the three major areas that Americans believed would cause things to improve.

Science, medicine, and education have never prevented wars, eliminated poverty, stamped out prejudice or crime. These are not the answers because the real problems are not addressed, only the "presenting" problems. The heart of the problem is man's basic nature. This is discussed further in Chapter 3.

WHY STUDY PROPHECY?

Understanding the future is one reason to study prophecy. Other reasons include the following:
1. Through the study of prophecy, we see that God is in control of this world.
2. Many books in the Bible are devoted to prophecy, so God must feel it is important. If it is important to God, it should be important to us.

3. Prophecy helps confirm the Bible's authority. For example, there are prophecies in the Old Testament which are fulfilled in the New Testament. When we read prophecies about the future, such as the rapture, tribulation and Antichrist, we know that God is working through events in accordance with His will.
4. The study of prophecy brings assurance to the true believer in Jesus Christ. Since God was faithful to fulfill past prophecies, we can trust Him to fulfill future prophecies. No matter how bad things look, we know that God is ultimately in control.
5. The study of prophecy produces a holy life. New Testament references to the Second Coming of Christ usually include an exhortation to godliness (Titus 2:11-13).[3]

BIBLICAL RELIABILITY

The reliability of the Bible as the infallible Word of God is the essential foundation stone for the Christian message. Strong evidence is essential so that we can "give an account for the hope that is in you (us), yet with gentleness and reverence" (I Peter 3:15). The Bible tells us to be prepared to defend our faith.

There are numerous books on apologetics (or defense of the Christian faith). One defense is the uniqueness of the Bible. Josh McDowell, a well known Christian author in the area of apologetics, discusses some of the characteristics that establish the Bible's uniqueness. The Bible was written over a period of 1,500 years, covering 40 generations, and written by 40 authors from every walk of life. The authors include: fishermen, poets, kings, peasants, statesmen and scholars. Furthermore, the Bible was written from different places (wilderness, dungeon, palace, prison, isle of Patmos); it was written at different times (times of war and peace). It was written from three continents (Asia, Africa, Europe), and in three languages (Hebrew, Aramaic, Greek).[4]

Josh McDowell, in *Evidence that Demands a Verdict*, not only discusses the Bible's uniqueness, but also provides a comprehensive defense of the Christian faith. He said that while the above points do not prove the Bible is the Word of God, "to me it proves that it is unique ('different from all others; having no like or equal'). A professor remarked to me: 'If you are an intelligent person, you will read the one book that has drawn more attention than any other, if you are searching for the truth.'"

The Bible can be defended in the following ways: archeologically, historically, prophetically, and philosophically. One example is the historical evidence of a great worldwide flood. A biologist and dean of science said "there are more than 500 accounts of vast primordial floods from cultures all over the world. Some scientists think the stories have a factual basis. Scientists agree that major extinctions of animals occurred about 11,500 years ago. Palmer reports that North America lost three-fourths of its large animals; devastation was even worse in other parts of the globe. What accounted for these deaths?"[5]

Even in the age of computers, we have evidence of the reliability of the Bible. Does proof exist to authenticate any miracle in the Bible? Scientific proof does exist, as shown in the next section.

Missing Day

On May 1, 1971, Bob Gooding of "Contact 8," Channel 8 News, read the following article entitled "The Missing Day."

> It concerns a missing day in time discovered and related by Harold Hill, president of the Curtis Engine Company in Baltimore, Maryland and a consultant in the space program. Mr. Hill stated that he thought one of the most amazing things that God has for us today happened to our astronauts and space scientists at Green Belt, Maryland. They were trying to determine the

The Real Prophet

position of the sun, moon and planets 100 years and 1000 years from now. In order to do this, they had to plot the orbits through past centuries. They ran the computer measurement back and forth over the centuries and suddenly it came to a halt. The computer signaled that there was something wrong either with the information fed into it or with the results compared to the standards. They called in the service department to check it out and found nothing technically wrong. The computer still came up with the same discrepancy . . . a day was missing in space in elapsed time. The scientists were dumbfounded. There was no answer.

One of the team remembered a reference to the sun standing still in the Bible. Upon checking, they found in the Book of Joshua a pretty "ridiculous" statement for anybody who has "common sense." According to the Scripture, Joshua was concerned because he was surrounded by the enemy and if darkness fell, they would overpower him, so Joshua asked the Lord to make the sun stand still. "So the sun stood still in the midst of heaven, and hasted not to go down about a whole day." (Joshua 10:13). There was the missing day!

They checked the computers going back to the time it was written and found it was close but not close enough. The elapsed time that was missing back in Joshua's day was 23 hours and 20 minutes . . . not a whole day. They again read the passage and there it said, "about [approximately] a whole day." This still did not account for the other missing 40 minutes. The 40 minutes had to be found because in projecting spacial orbits, it would be multiplied many times over.

Again, the man remembered somewhere in the Bible that it said the sun went backwards. In Second Kings, Chapter 20, Hezekiah, on his deathbed, was visited by the prophet Isaiah who told him that he was not going to die. Hezekiah did not believe him and

> asked for a sign as proof. Isaiah said, ". . . shall the shadow go forward ten degrees or back ten degrees?" Hezekiah replied, "It is a light thing for the shadow to go down ten degrees: nay, but let the shadow return backward ten degrees" (2 Kings: 20:9-10). Ten degrees is exactly 40 minutes!
>
> Twenty-three hours and twenty minutes in Joshua plus forty minutes in Second Kings, make the missing twenty-four hours the space travelers had to log in the logbook as being the missing day in the universe.

Prophecy is one of the major ways the Bible is unique and is set apart from other religious books. Only the God of the Bible has the ability to foretell the future with 100% accuracy through His prophets. No other "god" or supernatural force has that ability.

The Bible is the only volume produced by an individual or group of individuals which contains many prophecies relating to Israel, to certain cities, to all the people worldwide, and to the coming of the Messiah. In the ancient world, many devices were used to determine the future through divination. In all Greek and Latin literature, we cannot find a specific prophecy of a great historical event to come in the future, nor is there a prophecy of a Savior to arise in the human race.[6]

Prophet or Fraud?

If prophecy sets the Bible apart from all other manuscripts as infallible, what sets the prophet apart from a fraud, a psychic, or a fortuneteller? There has to be a way to distinguish the true prophet of God from all others.

One way to begin is to examine what God said to Moses.

> And it shall come about that whoever will not listen to My words which he shall speak in My name, I Myself will require it of him. But the prophet who shall speak

> a word presumptuously in My name which I have not commanded him to speak, or which he shall speak in the name of other gods, that prophet shall die.
> And you may say in your heart, "how shall we know the word which the Lord has not spoken?" When a prophet speaks in the name of the Lord, if the thing does not come about or come true, that is the thing which the Lord has not spoken. The prophet has spoken it presumptuously; you shall not be afraid of him (Deuteronomy 18:19-22 NASB).

"This teaches us that the true prophet had to predict some things that would take place in his lifetime so that his authenticity could be verified."[7] From this we can make the following observations:
1) If a prophet speaks something that doesn't come true, he has spoken "presumptuously." What he has spoken is not from God and he is not to be feared.
2) If a prophet speaks presumptuously and it is not in "My name" (God's name) or is "in the name of other gods, that prophet shall die." The test of a true prophet of God is very simple. It leaves no room for error or guessing. He has to have a 100% success rate or he dies.

Throughout history and in our day, many so-called "prophets" have lived and have written books. Some "prophetic" sources and individuals who have declared themselves "prophets" include: Jean Dixon, Edgar Cayce, Nostradamus, Mayan Calendar interpreters, Hopi Indian prophecies, New Age prophets, palm readers, astrologers, tarot card readers and channelers. None has an accuracy rating comparable to the prophets of the Bible. In Biblical times, these so called "prophets" needed to have a 100% accurate record. If not, they were cast out as false prophets, had their writings burned or were stoned to death.[8]

One requirement is 100% accuracy. However, a prophet may predict events accurately (although not 100%), but not necessarily be from God. "Deuteronomy 18 – claims that what does not become fulfilled is not true prophecy. It should be remembered that this is a negative criterion. Thus, what does become fulfilled is still not necessarily from God. When a false prophet makes a fulfilled prediction, this may be a test of God's people. Deuteronomy 13 deals theologically with and strikes a clear and ringing blow; if the prophet uses other gods removed from the true God (V.2), then he is obviously not of Yahweh."[9]

Besides 100% accuracy, there are two questions to consider about a true prophet. Is he merely guessing (a fraud)? Or is he prophesying from another "god" or supernatural being (demonic)?

The criteria to test the prophet are clearly identified in the Bible. The messages we have received through New Age psychics or the occult cannot be 100% supported by empirical evidence. When they are accurate, it is either guesswork or they are fed information from a demonic being.

God dwells in eternity outside of the confines of time according to Isaiah 57:15. "But how does He authenticate His message to us? How does He assure us that the message really comes from Him and is not a fraud or a contrivance? One way is to demonstrate that the message has its source from outside our time domain. God declares, 'I alone know the end from the beginning' (Isa. 46:10). His message includes history written in advance. We call this 'prophecy.'"[10]

Many Biblical prophecies were written several hundred years before Christ and were fulfilled both in the Old Testament as well as during the time of Jesus. It is important to look at some of the many Old Testament prophecies that were fulfilled in history.

OLD TESTAMENT PROPHECIES

Some of the Old Testament prophecies that were fulfilled in history include:
1) Destruction of the City of Tyre. Ezekiel 26:3,4,7,8,12,14,21 (592-570 B.C.)

2) Destruction of Sidon. Ezekiel 28:22-23 (542-570 B.C.)
3) Destruction of Samaria. Hosea 13:16 (748-690 B.C.); Micah 1:6 (738-690 B.C.)
4) Destruction of Gaza – Ashkelon. Amos 1:8 (775-750 B.C.); Jeremiah 47:5 (626-586 B.C.); Zephaniah 2:4,6,7 (640-621 B.C.)
5) Destruction of Moab – Ammon. Ezekiel 25:3-4 (592-570 B.C.); Jeremiah 48:47 (626-586 B.C.), 49:6
6) Destruction of Petra and Edom. Isaiah 34:6,7,10,13-15 (783-704 B.C.); Jeremiah 49:17-18 (626-586 B.C.); Ezekiel 25:13-14 (592-570 B.C.); Ezekiel 35:5-7
7) Destruction of Thebes and Memphis. Ezekiel 30:13-15 (592-570 B.C.)
8) Destruction of Nineveh. Nahum 1:8,10; 2:6; 3:10,13,19 (661-before 612 B.C.)

These are just a few examples of prophecies made several hundred years before Christ that were fulfilled in history.[11] Josh McDowell lists four more Old Testament prophecies and their fulfillment in his book *Evidence that Demands a Verdict*.

One obvious truth that stands out in the study of prophecy is God's direct influence throughout history. The prophets could not control the fulfillment. They made no claim from their own authority. They were the prophets and God was responsible for the fulfillment of the judgments.[12]

God is a merciful and patient God, but He is also a just God. He prophesied judgment on cities and nations and these prophecies were fulfilled. He prophesied a great judgment over the whole earth (Matthew 24:3-44; Mark 13:3-32; Luke 21:25-33; I Thes. 5:2-3; II Thes. 2:2-12; Rev. 6-19), which will be fulfilled.

Alexander the Great: an Important Figure in Prophetic History

Daniel prophesied four great world empires. The first world empire was Babylon followed by the Media-Persian empire, then the Greek empire, followed by the Roman empire. Alexander the Great ushered in the Greek empire. Prior to the rise of Alexander, Greece was divided into five tribes which spoke different dialects and were too busy fighting each other to become a great empire.

Alexander, a genius tutored by Aristotle, was fathered by a warrior king from the tribal state of Macedonia. His mother was disliked by his father; she was devoutly occultic. His mother's survival depended upon Alexander's success. She taught Alexander that he was much more than a mere man. The driving force in his life was a result of his own vision of personal greatness.[13]

Alexander learned battle tactics from his father who was later killed by an assassin, which thrust the eighteen-year-old Alexander into a mighty leadership role. He ingeniously devised new battle strategies and quickly learned how to keep his enemy off balance. He conquered all the other Greek tribes and united them into one nation. He also developed one common language. "Since they spoke in five dialects, Alexander knowing that exact communication was essential in battle, fused together the best of the dialects and made one common language. . . . This dialect was named Koine Greek, which means 'Common Greek.' Alexander commanded all the tribes to learn 'common language.'"[14]

Within two years, Alexander had Greece united and ready for conquest. Through clever psychological and military training, he had the Greek army capture Persia, the second world empire in 331 B.C.

Following the downfall of the Persian Empire, Alexander employed an unusual tactic. Instead of making the Persians slaves, he made friends with them. He required them to learn the Greek language and to embrace the Greek culture. Providentially, God accomplished His purpose through Alexander by making Koine Greek the universal language.[15]

Greek – A Providential Language

The original manuscript of the New Testament was written in Koine Greek, a creation of Alexander the Great. During the time of Christ, the Roman Empire was in power, but the universal language was Koine Greek.

The Old Testament was written in Hebrew, and later was translated into Greek, known as the Septuagint (or LXX) for the Seventy Translators. The Greek translation was completed in 165 B.C. To understand why this translation took place, we have to return to the scene of Alexander's conquests.

Hal Lindsey, a well-known author in the area of prophecy, relates the historical account of the translation of the Septuagint. During the time of Alexander's conquest, he made his move to conquer Jerusalem. A Jewish High Priest met with Alexander and explained how his life and career were prophesied in the second, seventh, and eighth chapters of Daniel. As a result, Alexander spared Jerusalem, and took many of the royal family of Judah to become administrators over his kingdom. These Hellenized Jews needed a Greek translation of their Hebrew Bible. As a result, we have the Septuagint.[16]

God used Alexander the Great, from a pagan background, to create a language; his encounter with a Jewish High Priest resulted in a Greek translation of the Hebrew Bible. The Bible was now available to the Gentile world. "Thus, long before his birth, there were now available for the Gentile world the prophecies of the Messiah's coming as a humble servant who would provide a way to God for all peoples."[17]

Our God has sovereign control over people, events, and history. He has to transcend time and space (as we know it) to have control over it. What a great and awesome God we have!

Judgment on Israel

The Jewish people are, in themselves, evidence of the inspiration of the Bible.

When Frederick the Great asked a preacher one time for proof of the inspiration of the Bible, the preacher replied, "The Jew, your Majesty." The emblem of the Jewish nation is a bush burning unconsumed.

Why did God preserve this nation? It is because He has a great plan for them. Here are several reasons:
1) The Jewish race was raised up to teach that there is only one God. In the days of Abraham, the world was given over to idolatry and paganism. But the Jews have been the teachers of monotheism to the nations (one God).
2) This nation was raised up to be the writers and preservers of the scriptures (Romans 3:1,2).
3) This nation was preserved so that God could give the world a Savior through them (Jesus was a Jew).[18]

The nation of Israel has remained a nation against all the odds. It was conquered and destroyed in 606 B.C. by Babylon. Although the captives of Israel were allowed to return to their land and rebuild Jerusalem, it did not become a sovereign nation until May 14, 1948.

The Old Testament predicted the destruction of Israel and the scattering of the Jews among the nations. Because of Israel's idolatry and disobedience, they were judged. Consider the following Old Testament prophecy:

> I will lay waste your cities as well, and will make your sanctuaries desolate; and I will not smell your soothing aromas. And I will make the land desolate so that your enemies who settle in it shall be appalled over it. You, however, I will scatter you among the nations and will draw out a sword after you, as your land becomes desolate and your cities become waste (Lev. 26:31-33 NASB).

This prophecy was fulfilled starting with the Babylonian captivity.

The final destruction of the rebuilt Jerusalem (which was still not an established sovereign nation), happened in 70 A.D. by Titus and the Roman army. There are Old Testament and New Testament (by Jesus) prophecies concerning the destruction of Jerusalem and the Temple. The following Old Testament prophecies are examples of these predictions.

> The Destruction of the Temple "... and the Lord, whom you seek, will suddenly come to His Temple..." Malachi 3:1. This verse along with four others (Psalms 118:26; Daniel 9:26; Zechariah 11:13; Haggai 2:7-9) demands that the Messiah come while the Temple of Jerusalem is still standing. This is of great significance when we realize that the temple was destroyed in 70 A.D. and has not since been rebuilt![19]

The following prediction in the book of Daniel lays out the chronology and timing of the crucifixion and destruction of Jerusalem and the Temple.

"Then after the sixty-two weeks the Messiah will be cut off and have nothing, and the people of the prince who is to come will destroy the city and sanctuary..." Daniel 9:26.

This is a remarkable statement! Chronologically:
1) Messiah comes (assumed)
2) Messiah cut off (dies)
3) Destruction of City (Jerusalem) and sanctuary (the temple).

The city and temple were destroyed by Titus and his army in 70 A.D.; therefore either the Messiah has already come or this prophecy was a lie.[20]

In the New Testament, Jesus prophesied the destruction of the temple approximately forty years before it happened. In reference to the temple, He said, "Do you not see all these things? Truly I say to you, not one stone here shall be left upon another, which will not be torn down" (Matthew 24:2 NASB). In Luke, He made the same prophecy and gave the reason for the destruction of the temple: the Jews' rejection of the Messiah. "For the days shall come upon you when your enemies will throw up a bank before you, and surround you, and hem you in on every side, and will level you to the ground and your children within you, and they will not leave in you one stone upon another, because you did not recognize the time of your visitation" (Luke 19:43-44 NASB).

Fulfillment of the Judgment of Israel

These Old and New Testament prophecies were literally fulfilled when Jerusalem was taken in 70 A.D. When Jesus was crucified, the Jews said, "His blood be on us and our children" (Matthew 27:25). A Roman army of 100,000 in 70 A.D. under Titus destroyed the Temple and the city. The city was defended by 90 towers and the siege lasted 4 months. Within the city was famine. Mothers killed and ate their babies (Deuteronomy 28:52-53). Many fled from the city, but were caught and crucified. The Romans swarmed around the Temple. Titus commanded his soldiers to spare the Temple, yet one soldier threw a blazing torch through a doorway, and the Temple was burned, leaving nothing but the rock upon which it stood. "On this rock today is a Mohammedan Mosque (Mosque of Omar). Josephus said 1,000,000 perished and 97,000 were taken captive. So, God scattered His people because they dishonored His name (Ez. 36:17-19), and crucified His Son. . . . Has God forgotten His people? No (Rom. 11:1,2,25,26). He has set them aside."[21]

After over 2,000 years of persecution and dispersion among the Gentile nations, Israel was reborn. God will restart the Jewish time clock as shown in Daniel's prophecy of 70 weeks.

Daniel's 70 Weeks: A Phenomenal Prophecy

The seventy week prophecy is found in Daniel 9:24-27 and is probably one of the most important prophecies in history. It is a prophecy about God dealing with the Jewish nation.

Hal Lindsey, in *Planet Earth: The Final Chapter*, refers to the 70 week prophecy of Daniel 9:24-27, as a view of Jewish history from Daniel's day until the return of Jesus Christ. Lindsey explains the Jewish measurement of time. In the same way the Greeks use "decade" for a period of ten years, the Hebrews use "shabua" or week for a period of seven years. Seventy of those "weeks" would represent a period of 490 years. This is a 70 week (or 490 year) prophecy concerning the Jews and the Holy City, Jerusalem.[22]

The historical background helps us understand Daniel's 70 weeks prophecy. The Babylonians captured and deported Daniel as a teenager. While in captivity and reading the prophecies of Jeremiah, Daniel understood that the 70 year captivity was about to end. He then committed himself to prayer. During this prayer, the angel Gabriel gave him the most remarkable prophecy in the Bible, the 70 week prophecy.[23]

The seventy-week prophecy (70 x 7 = 490 years) in Daniel was in regard to the Jewish nation. "Seventy weeks have been declared for your people . . ." (Dan. 9:24). The blessings or items to be completed are:
1) To finish the transgressions
2) Make an end of sin
3) Make atonement for iniquity
4) To bring in everlasting righteousness
5) To seal up vision and prophecy
6) To anoint the most holy place.[24]

The six promised blessings are related to the two works of the Messiah: His death and His reign. The first three have special reference to the sacrifice of the Messiah, which anticipate the establishment of His reign."[25]

The seventy "sevens" are divided into three categories of prophecy. The first category is seven weeks of seven (forty nine years), then sixty two weeks of seven (four hundred and thirty-four years) and the final week of seven (seven years). The entire prophecy period covers 490 years.

How do we calculate a year? When determining the length of the years, we rely on the 360-day year in Scripture. "The calendar year used in the Scriptures must be determined from the Scriptures themselves.
1) Historically – Compare Genesis 7:11 with Genesis 8:4, and the two of these with Genesis 7:24 and Genesis 8:3.
2) Prophetically – Many Scriptures refer to the great tribulation under various terms, but all have the common denominator of a 360-day year."[26]

What is the beginning point of this great prophecy? According to Daniel 9:25, the 70 week calendar began with "the issuing of a decree to restore and rebuild Jerusalem. . . . "

There are several decrees that had to do with the restoration of the Jews from the Babylon captivity. "However, in all these permission was granted for the rebuilding of the Temple and nothing was said about the re-building of the city."[27] These decrees did not fit the necessary requirements of the passage. "When we turn to the decree of Artaxerxes, made in his twentieth year, recorded in Nehemiah 2:1-8, for the first time is permission granted to rebuild the city of Jerusalem. This, then, becomes the beginning of the prophetic time appointed by God in this prophecy."[28]

How do we determine the date of this decree of Artaxerxes? According to Nehemiah 2:1, this decree was made "in the month of Nisan, in the twentieth year of King Artaxerxes . . . ." "There is no date specified, so according to the Jewish custom, the date is understood as the first day of the month, which would be Nisan 1, 444 B.C. March 5, 444 B.C. is our corresponding calendar date."[29]

The first 69 weeks terminated when Christ presented Himself to Israel as the Messiah. The time calculation is precise. From the edict to rebuild Jerusalem to the coming of the Messiah is 483 years (69 x 7). Each year is a Jewish prophetic year of 360 days or a total of 173,880 days.

This time period is equal to 476 solar years. Each solar year has 365 days in it. H. Hoehner describes the calculations as follows. "By multiplying 476 by 365.24219879 or by 365 days, 5 hours, 48 minutes, 45.975 seconds (there are 365 1/4 days in a year), one comes to 173,855 days, 6 hours, 52 minutes, 44 seconds, or 173,855 days. This leaves only 25 days to be accounted for between 444 B.C. and A.D. 33. By adding the 25 days to March 5 (of 444 B.C.), one comes to March 30 (of A.D. 33), which was Nisan 10 in A.D. 33. This is the triumphal entry of Jesus into Jerusalem."[30] This covers the period of time between 444 B.C. and A.D. 33.

Chart 1 is a representation of Daniel's 70 weeks prophecy. See note 31 for sources of additional charts regarding this prophecy.

Daniel's prophecy has taken us through 483 years or 69 weeks of the prophecy. The destruction of the City (Jerusalem) and the sanctuary (temple) was prophesied to occur after the crucifixion of Christ. ". . . Messiah will be cut off (crucified) and have nothing, and the people (Romans) of the prince to come (Antichrist) will destroy the city (Jerusalem) and the sanctuary (temple). And its end will come with a flood; even to the end and there will be war; desolations are determined." Daniel 9:26 (NASB) (Material in parenthesis by author).

The destruction of Jerusalem and the temple by the Romans, under the leadership of Titus was predicted by Daniel 9:26 and by Jesus in Matthew 24:2, Mark 13:2, and Luke 21:24. This prophecy was literally fulfilled. Sixty nine weeks of the 70 weeks have been fulfilled.

This brings us to the final week or seven years in this prophecy. There is a great time interval between the 69th and 70th week. This interval has lasted for over 1900 years and includes the present Church Age. This is a mystery in the Old Testament. It is alluded to, but not clarified until the New Testament.

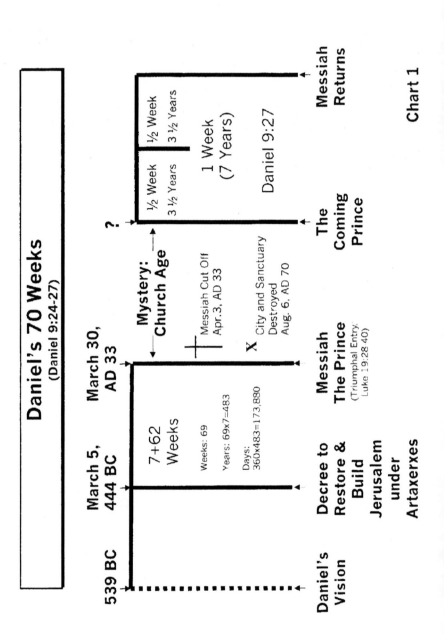

MYSTERY OF THE CHURCH AGE

To understand Biblical prophecy, one must understand that Israel and the Church are on different time clocks. "It seems that the Lord deals with Israel and the Church mutually exclusively. A chess clock, with its two interlocked representations, is an illustrative example; one clock is stopped while the other is running."[32]

The Church Age is a mystery hidden in the Old Testament. Paul said, "To me, the very least of all saints, this grace was given, to preach to the Gentiles the unfathomable riches of Christ, and to bring to light what is the administration of the **mystery which for ages has been hidden in God,** who created all things; in order that the manifold wisdom of God might now be made known through the Church to the rulers and the authorities in heavenly places" Ephesians 3:8-10 (NASB).

The Church Age can be viewed as a parenthesis in God's plan for Israel. This does not imply that God decided at the last minute to set Israel aside. It was a mystery alluded to in the Old Testament and revealed in the New Testament.

The Messiah is referred to in Isaiah 53 " as a lamb led to slaughter " (verse 7), and as Someone who would die for our sins ". . . He himself bore the sin of many, and interceded for the transgressors" (verse 12). He is also referred to as a mighty king. "For a child will be born to us, a Son will be given to us; and the government will rest on His shoulders; and His name will be called Wonderful Counselor, Mighty God, Eternal Father, Prince of Peace" (Isaiah 9:6). In this one verse, we have the birth of Christ prophesied in line one and His reign in line two. An unspoken time gap exists between the first line and the second line which says "the government will rest on His shoulders." The events of line two do not happen until the Second Coming of Christ when He ushers in the 1000-year millennial kingdom where Christ will reign (Revelation 20:6).

The Messiah was described in the Old Testament as a "suffering servant" or "lamb," and also as king or "Mighty God" and

"Prince of Peace." These two roles of Jesus the Messiah are similar to seeing two mountains from a distance with an unseen valley between them. The unseen valley is the Church Age, a truth hidden in the Old Testament and revealed in the New Testament.[33]

God works differently with Israel than He does with His Church. This difference is an important piece of the puzzle that helps us interpret and unlock the prophetic puzzle. It actually illuminates prophecy, especially in light of our current world status.

The 70th week in Daniel or the final seven years is the tribulation period. It is a time of judgment upon the world. This final period of time, when Israel's clock starts ticking again, begins with a seven year covenant or treaty between the Antichrist and the nation of Israel (Daniel 9:26-27). In verse 26, "the prince to come" refers to the future Antichrist. Verse 27 says, ". . . he will make a firm covenant with the many for one week;" the "many" refers to Israel (as shown in verse 24). "Seventy weeks have been declared for your people. . . ." Daniel's people refers to the nation of Israel. The "prince to come" cannot refer to "Messiah the Prince" in verse 25, because it refers to the future and "he" is associated with evil "abominations."

JESUS CHRIST – THE FULFILLMENT OF OLD TESTAMENT PROPHETS

The literal fulfillment of the Old Testament prophecies demonstrates the accuracy and reliability of the Bible. "The fact of fulfilled prophecy is found in the Bible alone; hence it presents proof of Divine inspiration that is positive, conclusive, and overwhelming. Here is the argument in brief: no man, unaided by Divine inspiration, foreknows the future, for it is an impenetrable wall, a true 'iron curtain' to all mankind. Only an almighty and all-knowing God can infallibly predict the future."[34]

Jesus Christ was the Messiah that Israel longed for, but did not accept. In Corinthians, Paul said, "But we preach Christ crucified, to Jews a stumbling block . . ." (I Corinthians 1:23 NASB). The Jews were looking for a mighty king to rule over them. Remember the mountain peaks? They rejected Jesus as a "lamb" to die for their sins. They were looking for the second mountain peak, which will be revealed in the future.

Israel rejected Jesus as their Messiah. As a result they were temporarily set aside, but not rejected. "I say then, God has not rejected His people, has He? May it never be!" (Romans 11:1 NASB). The Lord will again deal with the nation of Israel in Daniel's 70th week, the tribulation period.

The Old Testament contains many predictions of the Messiah that only Jesus could fulfill and these prophecies were fulfilled in the Gospels. More than 400 years passed between the Messianic predictions of the Old Testament and their fulfillment in the Gospels. Many of the predictions were much older than 400 B.C. Predictions from Moses (1500 B.C.) to Malachi (400 B.C.) cover over 1100 years. During that time, a succession of prophets and predictions testified to the coming Messiah.[35]

When looking at fulfilled prophecy, it is inconceivable how anyone could not believe in the reliability of the Bible as the inspired Word of God. The fulfillment of specific, detailed prophecy validates the Bible and sets it apart from all other faiths. Many other world religions try to build their claims upon miracles that cannot be proven. There is no other religion in the history of the world that has ventured to frame prophecies and show their fulfillment.

CHANCE FULFILLMENT?

The probabilities of coincidence or chance fulfillment of these prophecies are minute.

> "Suppose," says Dr. Olinthus Gregory, "that there were only 50 prophecies in the Old Testament (instead of 333) concerning the first advent of Christ, giving details of the coming messiah and all meet in the person

of Jesus . . . the probability of chance fulfillment as calculated by mathematicians according to the theory of probabilities, is less than one in 1,125,000,000,000,000. Now add only two more elements to these 50 prophecies, and fix the time and the place at which they must happen and the immense improbability that they will take place by chance exceeds all the powers of numbers to express (or the mind of man to grasp)."[36]

BRIEF SUMMARY OF OLD TESTAMENT PROPHECIES FULFILLED IN CHRIST

1. He was to come from the tribe of Judah (Genesis 49:10); Fulfillment: Matthew 1:3, Hebrews 7:14.
2. He was to be born of a virgin (Isaiah 7:14); Fulfillment: Matthew 1:18-23.
3. He was to be born in Bethlehem (Micah 5:2); Fulfillment: Matthew 2:1; Luke 2:5-6.
4. He must come at a specific time in history (Daniel 9:24-25); Fulfillment: Luke 2:1.
5. He must be preceded by a forerunner (Isaiah 40:3); Fulfillment: Luke 1:17 and Matthew 3:1-3.
6. His ministry was to begin in Galilee (Isaiah 9:12); Fulfillment: Matthew 4:12, 16-23.
7. His ministry was to be characterized by miracles (Isaiah 35:5-6); Fulfillment: Matthew 11:4-6; John 11:47.
8. He was to be sold out for 30 pieces of silver (Zechariah 11:12); Fulfillment: Matthew 26:31-56.
9. His hands and feet were to be pierced (Psalm 22:16); Fulfillment: John 19:18,37; John 20:25.
10. He was to be buried with the rich in His death (Isaiah 53:9); Fulfillment: Matthew 27:57-60.

These 10 prophecies and their fulfillment in Christ barely scratch the surface of over 300 Old Testament prophecies. Just using these

10 prophecies – the odds against any man fulfilling these prophecies are astronomical. As we saw in Daniel 9:24-27 (70 week prophecy), the Messiah not only had to fulfill all of the other prophecies, He had to fulfill them at a specific time in history.

There can be no question that Jesus Christ was the Messiah who was crucified to pay the penalty for our sins. The accuracy and precision of those Old Testament prophecies could not have come from anyone other than God Himself.

In this chapter we have covered how a true prophet is determined, the fulfillment of some of the Old Testament prophecies, the fulfillment of messianic prophecies, and then briefly covered the Church Age and the amazing 70 week prophecy found in the book of Daniel. The remainder of this book involves a building process, pictured as a pyramid. We have established the foundation and the reliability of prophecy along with the extreme improbability of chance fulfillment. In the next chapter, we will look at reasons to believe that our Lord will return soon.

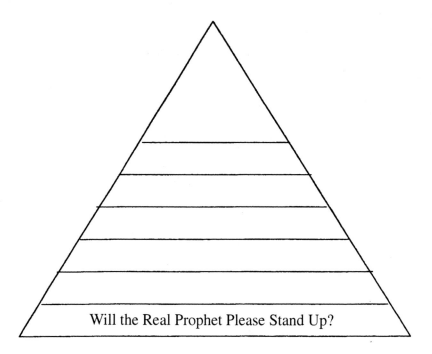

- TWO -

GENERATION X - THE LAST GENERATION?

"Truly I say to you, this generation will not pass away until all these things take place."
Matthew 24:34 NASB

This chapter reviews specific signs of the end times, including Israel and its pivotal role in God's prophetic plan. Historically, the nation of Israel has been under the domination of four major world empires. Israel was scattered among the Gentile nations and then miraculously reborn. We will see how this rebirth is related to the "parable of the fig tree" and the "last generation."

MIRACULOUS REBIRTH OF A NATION

Israel is the only nation destroyed for nearly 2,000 years and then re-established. Israel has not existed as a sovereign nation since the Babylonian conquest in 606 B.C. In the time of Christ, Jerusalem existed but under Roman rule. Israel was declared a sovereign nation in 1948.

The Old Testament predicted Israel's final destruction. A few of these predictions include:
- Palestinian cities will resemble waste (Leviticus 26:31,33)
- Desolation will come over the sanctuaries (Leviticus 26:31)
- Desolation will come over the land (Leviticus 26:32,33)
- Palestine will be inhabited by enemies (Leviticus 26:32)

- People of Israel will disperse (Leviticus 26:33)
- Jews will be persecuted (Leviticus 26:33).[37]

Jesus prophesied the final destruction of Jerusalem. In response to one of the disciple's comments about the temple, "Jesus said to him, 'Do you see these great buildings? Not one stone will be left upon another which will not be torn down'" (Mark 13:2). These predictions of Israel's destruction in both the Old Testament and the Gospels were fulfilled when the Roman army under Titus destroyed Jerusalem in 70 A.D. At present, the nation of Israel is still in the "Times of the Gentiles." Nebuchadnezzar's prophetic dream shows Israel in its historical context. This dream covers Israel under four world empires.

FOUR WORLD EMPIRES

The four world empires covered in the second chapter of Daniel include: the Babylonian Empire, the Medo-Persian Empire, the Greek Empire, and the Roman Empire. These four world empires span history from 606 B.C. to the Second Coming of Christ.

This great span of time is referred to in Scripture as the "Times of the Gentiles." Jesus refers to this time period in Luke 21:24 (NASB): "and they will fall by the edge of the sword, and will be led captive unto all the nations; and Jerusalem will be trampled underfoot by the Gentiles until the times of the Gentiles be fulfilled."

The final seven years of the "times and the seasons" for Israel coincide with the times of the Gentiles. The termination of the final seven years of judgment is identical for Jews and Gentiles, according to Daniel 9:24-27, 38.[38]

These four world empires are shown in Daniel 2. "Daniel saw an image of four successive world empires. In order, he saw Babylon fall to the Medo-Persian Empire, which fell to the Greek Empire, which fell to the Roman Empire. The prophet saw the destruction of each of the empires in detail – except Rome. From Daniel's perspective, Rome never ceases to exist, but is still in power on the day of the Lord."[39]

The continuity of Rome is especially important to the end times. Although the Roman Empire lost its authority, it never actually fell. The preceding three world empires fell, but not Rome. The Roman Empire lost its power and authority over the next two millennia, but remnants of its culture and authority have remained.[40]

The four world empires, also referred to as the "Times of the Gentiles," are represented by a great image in the dream of Nebuchadnezzar, the Babylonian king. Daniel interprets this dream by divine revelation for the king. This great image, found in Chapter 2 of Daniel, has parallel symbolism in Daniel 7 and 8, with images of ferocious animals. "Nebuchadnezzar sees Gentile dominion as man sees it (the nations in all their glory). But in Daniel 7 we will see how God sees Gentile dominion (ferocious animals devouring one another)."[41]

While the fourth empire, Rome, was not destroyed or overtaken, it will be destroyed in the future. Daniel 2:45 says, "Inasmuch as you saw a stone that was cut out of the mountain without hands and that it crushed the iron, the bronze, the clay, the silver, and the gold, the great God has made known to the king what will take place in the future. . . . " This verse shows the destruction of all the world empires including the ten kingdoms in the revived Roman Empire. Couple this with Daniel 7:12-14 which says, "as for the rest of the beasts, their dominion was taken away, but an extension of life was granted to them for a period of time. I kept looking in the night visions, and behold with the clouds of heaven one like a Son of Man was coming, and He came up to the Ancient of Days and was presented before Him. And to Him was given dominion, Glory and a kingdom. . . . " Scripture confirms that the image in Daniel or the "Times of the Gentiles" has not run its course, which history confirms.

Missler and Eastman give a brief overview of the history of the Roman Empire. Around A.D. 476, the Roman Empire broke up. Each of the pieces of the empire tried for global dominion without fully succeeding. The Dutch, French, German, Spanish,

Times of the Gentiles
Daniel 2 Compared with Daniel 7 and 8

DANIEL 2	DANIEL 7	DANIEL 8	EMPIRE	DATE
Head of Gold	Lion (7:4)		Babylonian (2:48)	626 B.C.
Chest and Arms of Silver	Bear (7:5)	Ram (8:3-4,20)	Medo-Persia (8:20)	539 B.C.
Belly and Thighs of Bronze	Leopard (7:6)	Male Goat (8:5,21)	Greece (8:21)	330 B.C.
Legs of Iron	Beast		Rome	63 B.C.
Feet of Iron and Clay				10 Kingdoms (Revived Roman Empire) (7:7-8)

and English attempted it, but never really succeeded as the Romans did.

Daniel suggested these "pieces" (Roman Empire) will recombine in the final empire. Many Bible scholars are looking for an ultimate revival of the Roman Empire.[42] Some suggest that the current moves within the European Union may be setting the stage for the final government.[43]

The image in Daniel is a picture of future things. History confirms the accuracy of Daniel's predictions. The books of Daniel and Revelation compliment each other. Daniel can be viewed as the ABC of prophecy just as Revelation may be viewed as the XYZ of prophecy.[44]

ISRAEL: GOD'S TIME PIECE

The nation of Israel serves as a pivotal nation in understanding prophecy. As previously discussed, the Old Testament prophets predicted the takeover of Israel and its scattering among the nations. They also predicted the re-gathering of Israel. "For I will take you from the nations, gather you from all the lands, and bring you into your own land" (Ezekiel 36:24 NASB). For over 2,500 years, this prophecy was not fulfilled.

This all changed on May 14, 1948. This event occurred approximately 2500 years after Babylon captured Jerusalem. "The Americans immediately recognized the State of Israel. The Russians also recognized the new state, not wanting to risk losing a possible client state in the region. Reluctantly, the United Nations accepted Israel's Declaration of Independence in accordance with the 1947 UN Partition Plan."[45]

The birth of the nation of Israel was also prophesied in Ezekiel 37. "Thus says the Lord God to these bones, 'Behold, I will cause breath to enter you that you may come to life. . . . Son of man, these bones are the whole house of Israel . . . " (Ezekiel 37:5,11 NASB). The establishment of Israel as a nation is as monumental as "bones coming to life." The rebirth of the nation of Israel is an extremely important prophetic fulfillment of Ezekiel 37 and 36:24. This begins the countdown to the final chapter in this present era (the Church Age). We turn now to Israel symbolized by a fig tree.

Parable of the Fig Tree

In Matthew 24:3, Jesus was asked by His disciples, "Tell us, when will these things be, and what will be the sign of Your coming and of the end of the age?" Jesus answered their questions by listing the signs first and then He gave the event in time preceding His Second Coming. He said: "Now learn from the parable of the fig tree: when its branch has already become tender, and puts forth its leaves, you know that summer is near" (Matthew 24:32 NASB). What does this verse mean and what does the fig tree symbolize? Hal Lindsey explains it as follows.

> The fig tree is a symbol for Israel today in much the same way the eagle symbolizes America or the bear is a symbol for Russia. . . . The Bible does refer to a fig tree some 33 times – 18 times in the Old Testament alone. In context, the fig tree is always a symbol for Israel . . . . Just as that is a sure sign the general time of summer has arrived, so, the argument goes, is the restoration of Israel to her land a sure sign the general time of Christ's return has arrived.[46]

This verse refers to a nation (Israel) symbolized by a fig tree; this assumes that Israel is in existence (which occurred in 1948). It also refers to a time ". . . puts forth its leaves, you know that summer is near" (Matthew 24:32 NASB).

This time reference is narrowed further by the next verse, Matthew 24:33: "even so you too, when you see all these things, recognize that He is near, right at the door." It is then narrowed still further: "Truly I say to you, *this generation* will not pass away until all these things take place" (Matthew 24:34 NASB) (italic added by author). In this passage, the word "generation" immediately follows the term "fig tree," which symbolizes Israel.

Jesus said the leaves would symbolize:
- Religious deception and occult practices
- Hot Wars and Cold Wars (wars and rumors of wars)
- International revolution among nations
- Ethnic conflicts
- Famines
- Earthquakes
- Plagues
- Global weather pattern changes
- Record killer storms

> Like the first leaves on the fig tree, they would all come at the same time. Like birth pangs, they would all increase in frequency and intensity.[47]

The generation alive at the time of the rebirth of Israel (1948) is the same generation that will be alive at the Second Coming of Christ. The number of years in a generation is not defined, but if your birth date is 1948 or later, you are in that generation. If you don't die of an accident or premature illness, you will be alive at the Second Coming of Christ.

SIGNS OF END TIMES

There are a number of end time signs that the Bible lists in different references. To understand what these signs mean, they have to be seen in their context as it relates to our current time. In addition to the signs previously mentioned, these include:
- False messiahs
- Persecution of Christians
- False prophets
- People's love grows cold

- Men fainting from fear
- The heavens shaken
- Falling away from sound doctrine
- Increased lawlessness
- Terrors
- Signs in the heavens
- Betrayal by relatives and friends
- Signs in the sun, moon, and stars
- Dismay among nations
- Roaring of the seas
- Sun will be darkened and moon will not give its light
- Increased travel or mobility
- Increased knowledge
- Apostasy
- Occult
- Seared over conscience
- Forbidding marriage
- Abstaining from foods
- Murder
- Sorcery
- Immorality
- Theft.[48]

This list includes things that are specific to the tribulation period whereas the other signs have appeared throughout history, but increase in intensity as the tribulation period and Second Coming draw closer in time.

The temptation in the "last days" is to say nothing has really changed and all continues as it always has. The Bible predicts this line of thinking. "Know this first of all, that in the last days mockers will come with their mocking, following after their own lusts, and saying, 'Where is the promise of His coming?' For ever since the fathers fell asleep, all continues just as it was from the beginning of creation" (II Peter 3:3-4 NASB).

Some distinct differences exist between the present time and 1,500 years ago, 500 years ago, or even 50 years ago. These distinct differences over the last 20 years and to a lesser extent over the last 20 - 50 years, will show us why we are surely in the "last days."

Birth Pangs

Wars, famines, plagues, and earthquakes have occurred for thousands of years. Why should we believe that these are signs of the Second Coming? What is different?

The Bible refers to the term "birth pangs" in at least three passages: Matthew 24:8; Mark 13:8; and I Thessalonians 5:3. Jesus said:

> Many will come in My name saying, "I am He!" and mislead many. And when you hear of wars and rumors of wars, do not be frightened; those things must take place; but that is not yet the end. For nation will rise against nation, and kingdom against kingdom; and there will be earthquakes in various places. There will also be famines. These things are merely the beginning of *birth pangs* (Mark 13:8 NASB).

Jesus compares the time sequence between His first and second comings to the gestation period a woman goes through before she gives birth. A closer look at the meaning of "birth pangs" is helpful to understanding Mark 13.

In the first trimester of pregnancy, the female's egg is fertilized, followed by cell division. Biological processes are occurring on a microscopic level in the early days following conception.

By the second trimester, the mother feels the first movement of the fetus. During this time period, the fetus is growing rapidly.

"Toward the middle of the last trimester (32-40 weeks of gestation), the mother starts to feel false labor pangs, called Braxton-Hicks contractions. However, 'the end is not yet ... All these are the beginnings of sorrows.' These false contractions are a warning sign that a birth is on the way, but a significant period of time is still left."[49]

When the mother begins to feel false labor pains, it is a sign that the actual birth is not far off. If she is wise, she will prepare in advance for the actual delivery.

Early birth pangs are similar to false labor pains. When true labor begins, the frequency and intensity of the contractions accelerate until the actual delivery.[50]

This analogy could be expanded by comparing the frequency and acceleration of the false labor pains to the years preceding the seven-year tribulation period. The tribulation period (70th week in Daniel) which lasts for seven years will be a horrible time of judgment on the whole world. It is ended by the Second Coming of our Lord Jesus Christ. There will be great joy for true believers in Jesus Christ as there is great joy for a mother when a child is born and her period of labor is completed. We turn now to the "signs" spoken of by Jesus.

Earthquakes

Earthquakes have always been with us, but not as frequent or severe as currently. "In the last 100 years there has been a dramatic increase in the frequency and intensity of earthquakes worldwide. In the last 15 years, in California alone, earthquakes have increased dramatically – with killer quakes, those greater than 6.0 on the Richter scale, increasing to unprecedented levels since 1980."[51]

Earthquakes, by themselves, do not tell us much as a sign of the return of Christ. However, when the number of major earthquakes increases exponentially, it is significant. "History shows that the number of killer quakes remained fairly constant until the 1950's – averaging between two to four per decade. In the 1950's,

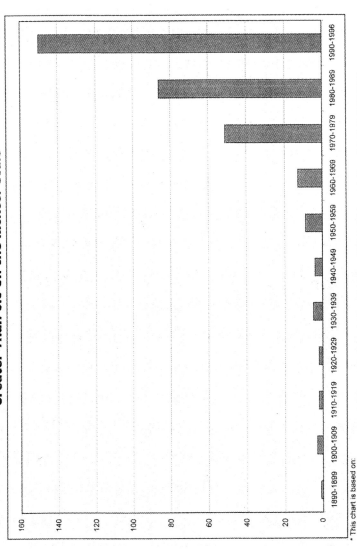

there were nine. In the 1960's, there were 13. In the 1970's, there were 51. In the 1980's, there were 86. From 1990 through 1996, there have been more than 150."[52]

From the decade of the 1950's with 9 earthquakes to the decade of the 1990's with 150+ earthquakes, the frequency has increased over 15 times in just 50 years.

"Skeptics argue that the increase in frequency of earthquakes is simply due to our improved ability to measure earthquakes worldwide. However, when this objection is carefully examined, it does not stand up. Since the 1960's the number of seismographs has been sufficient to detect any earthquake greater than 5.0 on the Richter scale occurring worldwide."[53]

Climate Changes

Weather changes have been significant over the last few years. Changes in climate threaten mankind's survival as well as the natural species and worldwide ecosystems.[54]

After the mid 70's and especially over the last decade, there has been a dramatic increase in storms, droughts, tornadoes, and floods. Nick Graham, a climate researcher at Scripps Institute of Oceanography in LaJolla, California, states that weather patterns became erratic after the mid-1970's. He noted dry falls and wetter winters; the climate changes were both local and worldwide.[55]

The weather has always been somewhat unpredictable, but what has been occurring are global weather changes. "A corollary consequence of the global warming will be storms of unprecedented destructive power. Records set by severe weather and its aftermath are presently occurring all over the world. This is what is unique about the global weather pattern changes that are now taking place."[56]

Global warming, the destruction of the rain forests, the deterioration of the ozone layer and other abuses have negatively affected the earth's ecosystems. "As of spring of 1997, the annual hole in the ozone layer has doubled. It is now computed to be twice the size of all of Europe. Animals in the southern part of Argentina have been found blind because of the effect of unfiltered sun rays on their eyes."[57]

Continued global warming, contributing to erratic weather patterns, will have devastating effects. "In 1995 experts monitored the worst, the most intense weather year in the history of recording weather events. There were more tornadoes, tropical storms, droughts, floods, and other extremes of weather combined in that year than experts had seen since recording began in the mid-1800's."[58]

In June of 2000, Joseph Hebert, an Associated Press writer, published an article on global warming forecast. The article stated the findings of the first-ever detailed national assessment of what could be expected to occur in the United States, if the warming trend continues over the next 100 years. ". . . [T]he assessment predicts entire ecosystems likely will shift northward as temperatures increase, and coastal areas will have to cope with higher sea levels and the prospect of more frequent storms, cities will swelter in more frequent heat waves, and droughts will become more likely in parts of the Midwest. . . . The warming will cause ocean levels to rise, causing barrier islands to disappear."

Global warming is increasing and will continue to cause changing weather patterns and to upset the world's delicate balance. Generally, scientists agree that temperatures are increasing as a result of greenhouse gases.[59]

Wars and Rumors of Wars

Wars have existed since the beginning of mankind. There have been many wars, including two world wars. What is different today? Like the analogy of the mother in labor, the answer lies in *frequency* and *intensity*. Now we add a third difference, *potential*.

The 20th century has been labeled by many the century of war and the bloodiest century of all history. At no time during this century has there been peace. At any one time in the 1990's there have been as many as 70 wars and regional conflicts being waged around the world. In recent years there have been more wars and devastation by wars, with several technologies now providing even greater opportunities for mass destruction.[60]

The frequency of wars has increased as well as the intensity and the devastation that has resulted from these wars. When Jesus made this prophecy in Matthew 24:7, He included two groups in conflict. "For nation will rise against nation, and kingdom against kingdom . . ." (Matthew 24:7 NASB). "What is rendered 'nation shall rise against nation' in text is generally adequate to convey the meaning intended. But a closer examination shows the Greek word translated "nation' is ethnos – the word from which we get the word ethnic. The word means 'a race, or tribe' – not an inconsistent definition for our modern understanding of ethnicity."[61]

Ethnic conflict is worldwide. We are continually bombarded by news of ethnic conflicts. Some examples of ethnic unrest include the former Yugoslavia with the tension between Serbs, Muslims and Croats. As a result of that conflict we have a new term, "ethnic cleansing," in place of "genocide."[62] Ethnic cleansing is more politically correct. As if relabeling something that is wrong, will somehow make it okay.

There are problems with ethnicity in India, Pakistan, Bangladesh, Sri Lanka, Algeria, and France. "Time magazine reported in an October 9, 1995, article, 'The Forgotten Wars,' that there were some 46 ethnic wars raging around the world right now."[63]

Riding on the heels of ethnicity is terrorism. When you combine terrorism with the nuclear potential present worldwide, we have an unpredictable monster on our hands. If one did not believe in

God and His promises to those who put their faith in Jesus Christ, the reality of the world's status would be terrifying.

Concerning our present world status, Missler and Eastman make the following statement:

> Currently, more than a dozen countries possess nuclear weapons, more than two dozen countries are building intercontinental ballistic missiles, and more than 60 countries have the technology to field a surface skimming cruise missile. And, they are all mad at each other. The cloud of imminent nuclear attack hangs over all foreign policy negotiations. The nightmare of a virtual wipe out of major civilizations remains only 30 minutes away. The unthinkable lurks behind every major strategic decision. The threat of nuclear terrorism is of great concern to the US State Department. By smuggling a device just smaller than a footlocker into the United States, terrorists could demolish a city the size of Los Angeles.[64]

In the future, there will be a World War III and the final battle will occur at Armageddon (Revelation 16:12-21). This will happen at the end of the tribulation period. Jesus will return before mankind completely destroys itself. This is the Second Coming of Christ (Revelation 19).

Billy Graham made the following statement concerning mankind's dilemma and man's solution:

> Pope John Paul II has stated, "Our future on this planet, exposed as it is to nuclear annihilation, depends on one single factor: humanity must make a moral 'about-face.'" But the question that confronts us is, how can this happen? Technologically, man has far exceeded his moral ability to control the results of his technology. Man himself must be changed.[65]

Billy Graham goes on to say that the change is possible through a spiritual renewal. The Bible teaches that man must undergo a spiritual rebirth (John 3:3).

Increase in Immorality and Violence

The increase in immorality and violence is obvious. What was acceptable in our culture in the 1990's and early 2000's, was not acceptable in the 1960's. Movies, television, and morality in general have declined drastically.

If you have been slowly desensitized by it, you may not have noticed it. "In the last 30 years there has been a 560 percent increase in violent crime. Illegitimate births have increased 419 percent. Divorce rates have tripled. The number of children living in single-parent homes has tripled. The teen suicide rate has increased 200 percent."[66]

The increase in immorality and violence has snowballed over the past thirty years. The numbers tell us there is a very real problem in our society. Things are not improving; they are deteriorating rapidly.

The killings at Columbine High School are one example of this, along with nine other school shootings. The following statistics show further evidence of increasing violence. Our per capita murder rate between 1975 and 1992 doubled; attempted murders have increased by seven times. The prison population has tripled.[68]

The crime rate (violent and nonviolent) in the latter part of the decade of the 1990's, decreased nationwide. "Nationally, the reasons given for the drop aren't too flattering to baby boomers. The nation's longest and steepest crime rise . . . came as baby boomers reached the crime prone ages of 15 to 25. The rate began to decline several years ago as people born right after World War II grew older and wiser" (Denton Record Chronicle, May 28, 2000, p. 1A).

While there are a number of possible reasons for this reduction in the crime rate, one is a shift in population and the crime-prone years. It would be erroneous to conclude that this reported crime drop is a result of an increase in morality and godliness.

We live in an immoral and violent time, but this is only the beginning of "birth-pangs." Immorality and violence will peak during the Tribulation Period (Revelation 9:21).

In one generation, we have undergone cultural deterioration. "We have gone from 'Ozzie and Harriet' to Ozzie Osborne, from 'Donna Reed' and 'Leave it to Beaver' to Marilyn Manson in one generation."[69]

Several years ago, Billy Graham said, "If God doesn't judge America soon, He would have to apologize to Sodom and Gomorrah."[70] Immorality is on the increase worldwide, not just in America.

Persecution of Christians

To the average American, the persecution of Christians may seem like a thing of the past, perhaps in early Christianity or in the Middle Ages. This is just not the case. There is worldwide persecution of Christians. This is another one of the signs preceding the return of the Lord (Matthew 24:9).

> Christians are already the most persecuted religious group in the world today, according to the international human rights group Freedom House. Eleven countries now practice systematic persecution of Christians, says Nina Shea, author of *In the Lion's Den*. . . . These eleven nations – and others that practice a more random brand of persecution – are dominated by one of two belief systems, communism or militant Islam.[67]

There are many examples of Christian persecution worldwide. International Christian Concern cites the following two examples of this.

1) There were two Christians who were arrested in Pakistan in 1998 on charges of blasphemy. The blasphemy involved an attempt to buy ice cream from a Muslim ice cream vendor. A report was filed by the vendor that slanderous remarks were made against Mohammed and Islam. According to Pakistan's Penal Code, if convicted they face mandatory execution.[71]
2) A 13 year-old daughter of a Christian Egyptian family was raped and kidnaped in March 1998 and forced by a terrorist group to convert to Islam. Later, the girl was released, but when she returned home, her family was attacked by the terrorists and were murdered by crushing their heads with stones and slitting open their bellies.[72]

Most Christians in America are not aware of the plight of our brothers and sisters in other countries. People who have studied Christian persecution over the ages tell us that a larger number of Christians have been martyred in the 20th century than the combined total of the past 19 centuries.[73]

FUTURE PREDICTIONS FROM A HUMAN PERSPECTIVE

This chapter has reviewed Biblical prophecies and several signs that precede the Second Coming of Christ. These signs have included:
- The uniqueness of Israel and re-establishment of the nation of Israel
- Numerous signs of the end times
- A review of the history and current status of earthquakes
- Weather changes
- Wars and rumors of wars
- Increase in immorality and violence
- Persecution of Christians.

Our focus has been on the geometric increase in both number and intensity. The re-establishment of Israel is a hallmark of the times, especially when considered in light of the other signs.

"Ironically, it is not just Bible prophecy students who see the world moving toward a climax. Lots of others agree – from Indian Shaman to secular scientists."[74] Any astute person who honestly looks at human history and the current state of our world would be hard pressed to be optimistic about the future of mankind.

There are already enough nuclear-tipped missiles on station and ready to launch to destroy civilization. "Dr. W. H. Pickering of Cal Tech confirmed this when he warned, 'in half an hour the East and West could destroy civilization.'"[75]

"In fact, if the Book of Revelation had never been written, some astute 20th century person might well predict these very catastrophes within this generation. And, of course, many who don't believe the Book of Revelation, or who are unfamiliar with it, are doing just that."[76]

We live in a high tech society with the nuclear capacity to destroy mankind. The world is a powder keg. If you ignore what the Bible says, if you are an atheist and therefore do not believe in the validity of prophetic fulfillment, the outlook for mankind is dismal.

"As Nathaniel Borenstein says, in the computer age, 'the most likely way for the world to be destroyed most experts agree is by accident. That's where we come in; we're the computer professionals. We cause accidents.'"[77]

A computer accident that destroys the world is a very real possibility. The possibility of a computer accident, with the existence of an arsenal of nuclear weapons, the increase in terrorist activities, and the moral decline of mankind, brings us to the edge of Armageddon.

Dr. George Wald, Nobel Prize winning scientist, Harvard University, made the following statement: "I think human life is threatened as never before in the history of this planet. Not just by one peril, but by many perils that are all working together and coming to a head at about the same time. . . . I am one of the scientists who finds it hard to see how the human race is to bring itself much past the year 2000."[78]

In conclusion, we must look at what Bible prophecy has said along with current events. If we view the world from God's perspective and the human perspective, the evidence points to this generation as the last generation.

This chapter reviewed Israel's place in history in relation to the four world empires and its rebirth as a nation. The "parable of the fig tree" was interpreted in light of the "last generation." The signs preceding the Second Coming of Christ were covered as viewed from a progressive or exponential standpoint.

Our first two chapters have reviewed the reliability of the Bible as confirmed by fulfilled prophecy. They have also shown Israel's place in prophecy as it relates to the signs of the Second Coming. This brings us to our next chapter which traces world views from man's perspective and then from God's perspective.

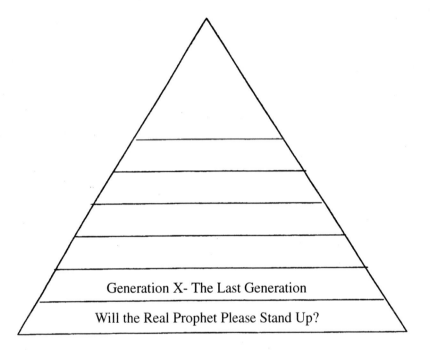

- THREE -

WORLD VIEW FROM HUMAN AND DIVINE PERSPECTIVES

"For as he [man] thinks in his heart, so is he."
Proverbs 23:7 NKJV

Prior to this chapter, the emphasis has been on prophecy and its fulfillment. The focus was God's prophetic Word, its historical fulfillment, and its future predictions.

The current chapter focuses on world views primarily from a human perspective and how that contrasts with God's perspective. A man's belief system is extremely important. We will see how the human mind is a battlefield in the supernatural realm.

MIND BENDERS

Great thinkers and philosophers have shaped man's thinking. Mankind is conditioned by the thoughts and ideas of influential people of the past who thought in terms contrary to Biblical principles.

Oftentimes, thought patterns and ideas contrary to God's word are very subtle. In most cases the deception is woven in with the truth.

To understand mankind's hostility toward God today, we must understand different world views and how they have changed over time. Philosophers have shaped our world views dramatically, especially over the last three hundred years.

"Classical philosophy was based upon the process of antithesis, which means that man thought in terms of cause and effect. This means if 'A' is true, then non-'A' cannot also be true. According to classical philosophy, values were absolute."[79]

Kant

Immanuel Kant was a German philosopher who lived in Prussia from 1724 to 1804. Before Kant, the world accepted classical philosophy, cause-effect relationships, and absolutes. Kant questioned whether a person could actually accept things beyond the five senses.

Kant went beyond realism by accepting the characteristics of both external and internal experience. "In Kant's analysis of the process of thought he proposed that no one can know anything except by experience."[80] He found no basis to accept absolutes. Kant's ideas triggered ideas for another German philosopher, Georg Wilhelm Hegel.

Hegel

Georg Hegel, (1770 - 1831), moved from antithesis (cause-effect) to synthesis. He believed that the outcome of one thought working against another produced a new thought. His approach to life left no room for absolutes.

Hegel opened the door to eliminating ultimate truth and the necessity of believing in a Creator God. Since Hegel's time, philosophy, morals, and even political thought have changed. Anyone who understands this development realizes that Hegel and synthesis have won.[81]

This shift in thinking is critical. It meant that the state did not have to obey moral laws. If nothing is absolute, everything is relative. Hegel "taught that the state did not have to obey moral laws, nor did governments have to keep their agreements. Hitler followed this philosophy to perfection."[82]

Kierkegaard

Soren Kierkegaard grew up in Denmark and lived from 1813 to 1855. His father was a rationalist who liked to invite theologians over for dinner and have rational debates with them. Kierkegaard rebelled against rationalism. He went to the opposite extreme and became the father of modern day existentialism.

Kierkegaard is considered the father of secular modern day thinking and modern theological thinking.[83] He built on Kant's emphasis on experience and Hegel's beliefs in relativity and came up with what he called a "leap of faith."

Kierkegaard left no room for reasoning and concluded that you could not arrive at a synthesis by the reasoning process. Truth was acquired by faith and experience through a "leap of faith." He was the father of both secular and religious existentialism.

Darwin

Charles Darwin was an Englishman (1809-1882), who lived in the nineteenth century. He gathered a vast amount of scientific information concerning plants and animals. After the accumulation of all his data, he devised a theory.

He developed a theory of "natural selection" and the "survival of the fittest." This theory is based on the belief that the earth cannot provide room and food for all its offspring. According to Darwin, the natural selection process is a result of competition which preserves life forms best suited for adaptation and survival. He believed lower forms struggle for existence to graduate to higher forms.[84]

Darwin then transferred his theories from plants and animals to man. The theory of evolution was born, a theory that contradicts the Biblical account of creation which states that God created man, animal, and plants "after their kind."

"If we accept the history of our evolution, then one fact stands out clearly: namely that we have arisen essentially as primate predators."[85] Man, according to Darwin, evolved and was not created.

"Hegel introduced the philosophical basis for man to see no necessity for a Creator God to whom man was responsible. The impact of this thought bomb is that since man had no special beginning, he has no special purpose or destiny. This thinking leads many to sink into amoral behavior, disorientation, and despair."[86]

CHANGING WORLD VIEW

This shift or evolving world view is one of despair starting with Hegel. Once we have disconnected from absolutes, we have disconnected from God, our Creator. We have lost our reference point. Francis Schaeffer, well-known Christian author, states the following. "Finite man in the external universe, being finite, has no sufficient reference point if he begins absolutely and autonomously from himself and thus needs certain knowledge. God gives us this in the Scriptures. With this in mind the scientist can understand, in their ultimate relationships, the truths that he is looking at."[87]

PSYCHOLOGY: A BRIEF HISTORICAL REVIEW

Throughout history, mankind has studied and devised theories to understand life, its meaning, and the nature of man. We have reviewed some of the ways that philosophers have affected our world view. The evolution of the study of psychology has also had an impact on our understanding of man.

Psychoanalysis

Sigmund Freud (1856-1939) was the founder of psychoanalysis. Freud was an atheist and was drawn to Darwin's theories

Changing World View
Philosophy

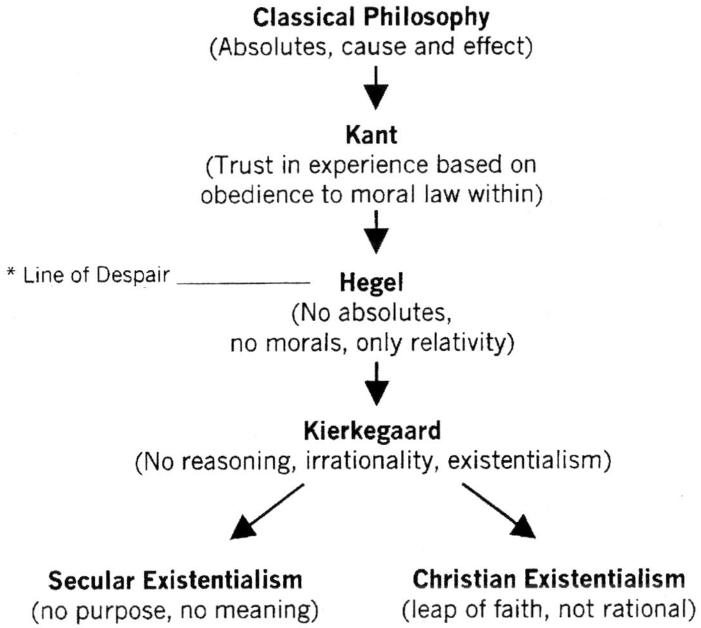

Classical Philosophy
(Absolutes, cause and effect)
↓

Kant
(Trust in experience based on
obedience to moral law within)
↓

* Line of Despair ———— **Hegel**
(No absolutes,
no morals, only relativity)
↓

Kierkegaard
(No reasoning, irrationality, existentialism)
↙ ↘

Secular Existentialism **Christian Existentialism**
(no purpose, no meaning)   (leap of faith, not rational)

---

* Chart based on information from Francis Schaeffer, *The God Who Is There* (Downers Grove, Ill.: InterVarsity Press, 1968) p. 21

Chart 4

because they showed promise of a great advancement in human knowledge.[88]

He put a heavy emphasis on the subconscious mind and determinism. Religion was considered unhealthy. Freud has had an enormous impact on psychology. He developed the concept of neurosis.

In a nutshell, the healing power of psychoanalysis lies in self-knowledge. If we, through psychoanalysis, know ourselves thoroughly and have access to our repressed unconscious, then healing will take place, according to Freud's theory.

Along with Freud's concept of psychoanalysis, comes exposure to his philosophy of life. "Freud's doctrines, and particularly his ethics, are the product of his concept of the human race. There is no purpose in man's existence. There is no goal in mankind's presence on earth. There is no God . . . and if this is so, all is permitted."[89]

Analytical Psychology

Carl Jung (1875-1961) developed analytical psychology. Jung goes beyond experience. He believed the mind consists of far more than the unconscious. "For Jung, however, there is a deeper, transpersonal unconscious, something that reflects the history of the human species and indeed the cosmic order, and which arises prior to an individual's experience. Within this collective unconscious are the so-called archetypes, which may be roughly defined as nuclear mythical themes (the Hero, the Great Mother, etc.)."[90]

Jung returns some emphasis to a form of spirituality. Philosophically he leans toward a synthesis or a One World Mind. This one world mind is an integral part of the current New Age philosophy, which we will discuss in a later chapter.

Existential Analysis

More popular in Central Europe, this approach mixed with some American strains of therapy and developed as the humanist psychology movement of the sixties.

Existential analysis broke away from the traditional approaches. According to Joel Kovel, existential analysis taps into our experience in a chaotic, godless world, without a belief system or a moral authority. It is a world that is taken for granted.[91]

In tracing psychological schools of thought, we begin to see similarities to some of the previous philosophical schools of thought. Existential analysis has thrown out morals and absolutes like Hegel and incorporated personal experience as our guide like Kierkegaard.

Humanistic Psychology: Human Potential Movement

This group includes different types of therapy as diverse as Rogerian psychotherapy, bioenergetics, encounter groups, and mystical therapy. The whole group tends to rally around existentialism and direct experience. "The fundamental principle is that man is the measure of all things."[92]

If man is the measure of all things, then man is a god. He alone becomes his own standard or reference point for morality and behavior.

In a relatively short period of time, man's world view is shifting from a God-centered external reference point to a man-centered internal reference point. The humanist claims that God has left the world and that man is free to elevate himself to God's level. It is a claim of unlimited potential.[93] As we will see in a later chapter, this fits in very neatly with the New Age concept of the evolution of consciousness or mind.

Rogerian Therapy

Carl Rogers, born in 1902, was both an existentialist and a humanist; he serves as a good representative of the humanist approach. His background helps shed light on belief in humanism.

Rogers was attending seminary for training in the ministry when he decided his calling was psychological counseling. Rogers believed that man is basically good and in his own words, "the facts are friendly." "In Rogers we see it as an intense belief in the goodness of man."[94]

If one follows this belief, he denies the dark side of man. Man only needs to self-actualize.

If man is basically good, then what is our problem? Why do we have wars? Why do we have prisons? Maybe Rogers lived in a world of peace. As far as I can tell from reading the newspaper and looking at Biblical prophecy, that age of peace has not yet arrived.

Mysticotranscendent Approach

These approaches to therapy move the person more toward altered states of consciousness. A religious aura surrounds their therapies. They include religious type approaches such as Zen Buddhism, Eastern religions, alpha-wave conditioning, yoga, and mind expanding drugs. "The transcendent approach becomes a religious one insofar as its altered state of consciousness is made meaningful, especially in the extent to which it may be said to correspond to some general truth about reality as against mere subjectivity."[95]

These approaches include mystical experience and border on the religious aspect. This movement into the mystical or experience once again takes us away from a Creator God who is personal and toward a transcendent experience possibly with a supernatural force that is "disguised as an angel of light" (II Corinthians 11:14 NASB).

There is not just one supernatural power in the universe. When people open themselves up to the supernatural (mystical, eastern religions, etc.), they need a reliable frame of reference. Humanism, where the person himself is the frame of reference, is totally unreliable due to man's subjective nature.

Behavioral Therapies

There are a number of behavioral therapies and techniques. Behavioral therapy in condensed form is the art of controlling human behavior through reward and punishment.

Behavioral therapy is very effective with animals and is effective with humans for some problems, but is limited. It has philosophical implications about the nature of man.

One of the most influential behavioral psychologists is B. F. Skinner. He believes the answers to man's problems come through manipulation of his environment. "The way to do it he thinks is through 'behavioral technology,' a developing science of control that aims to change the environment rather than people, that seeks to alter actions rather than feelings, and that shifts the customary psychological emphasis from the world inside men to the world outside them."[96] He believes that an "inner man is a superstition that originated, like belief in God, in man's inability to understand the world."[97]

Skinner's brand of therapy is deterministic and reduces man to the level of animals. This reflects Hegel's thinking (no absolutes, morals, or need for a Creator God) and Darwin's theory of evolution.

CHANGING WORLD VIEW - PSYCHOLOGY

Psychoanalysis (No God, no morals)
↓
Analytical Psychology (One world mind, synthesis)
↓

Existential Analysis (No absolutes, existentialism)
↓
Humanism (Man is a god, morals are relative)
↓
Rogerian (Man is good. Denial of sin)
↓
Mysticotranscendent approach (Goal is transcendence)
↓
Behavioral Therapy (Man is reduced to animal; God is eliminated)

It is obvious that the schools of psychology parallel the different philosophical schools of thought. Let's look at a quick review of the impact of philosophies on schools of psychology.

In psychoanalysis we can see the influence of Darwin and Hegel. Man is only a product of evolution and belief in God is unnecessary. To need a Creator God is a weakness.

In analytical psychology, we see an emphasis on experience yet Jung's theory has some religious overtones (collective unconscious, mythical themes) which are similar to Kant. Kant emphasized experience yet "obedience to a moral law within."

The philosophers Hegel and Kierkegaard directly and obviously influenced existential analysis. Truth is within and is not absolute but is found through personal experience.

Humanistic psychology was an offshoot of existential analysis adapted as an Americanized version. It involves a number of therapy schools including mystical therapy. One can see the influence of Hegel (no absolutes) and Kierkegaard (direct experience). Once absolutes are thrown out, God is thrown out and man becomes his own standard (or god).

Rogerian therapy fits into the humanist approach. Rogers believes man is innately good. If he is basically good, then why can't he be his own god?

The mysticotranscendent approach is existential with religious overtones. One can definitely see the existentialist Kierkegaard here. Remember Kierkegaard was the father of modern existentialism both secular and religious. Once again we run into the problem of a reference point. In this approach, the reference point is self and personal experience.

Behavioral therapy takes us back to Darwin. Humans are nothing more than evolved animals and have no Creator God. Again we can see Hegel's influence, no absolutes, man sets his own standards

PSYCHOTHERAPY PITFALLS

When looking at various limitations in psychotherapy approaches or solutions, one has to accurately diagnose the problem. Diagnosing the problem is built on one's view of man's nature and what is considered "normal."

Let's first look at the problem from a human point of reference. What is our standard? "It cannot be too strongly emphasized that changes can never be measured by some absolute standard, but only through the way a person evaluates his life. In other words, the 'better way' is the way one values."[98]

If there is no absolute standard, how do we determine mental illness? It is based on a norm of the majority of the population at a given point in time. People do not agree on the definition of mental health. It is difficult to find a group of psychiatrists who agree on a definition; it is impossible to find a criteria that people generally accept as a mental health definition.[99]

Psychiatrist Jerome Frank, professor emeritus at John Hopkins University School of Medicine, states: "The greater the number of treatment facilities and the more widely they are known, the larger the number of persons seeking their services. Psychotherapy is the only form of treatment which, at least to some extent, appears to create the illness it treats."[100]

To a limited extent, psychology can understand the root causes of mental illness and, therefore, can only treat them to a limited extent. When the problem is not really understood and is based on one or more psychological theories of personality, the solution (or treatment) is very questionable to say the least.

How does a psychotherapist determine if a patient is well? Is it because he or she feels better?

Once again, we need a standard to effectively diagnose and treat the whole person. In order to arrive at a standard, we need to understand man's nature.

MAN'S NATURE: AN UNDERSTANDING OF THE PROBLEM

In order to find a solution to a problem, it is essential to identify the problem accurately. We have touched on a few philosophers' and psychologists' views of our world. The approach to man's nature has originated from a human standpoint and not a divine one.

The development of psychological theories has originated from one or more philosophical schools of thoughts, which primarily originated in the 19th century. This search for truth using man as the reference point has proven futile.

According to the Bible, man is born with a sinful nature. Psalm 51:5 says, "Behold I was brought forth in iniquity, and in sin my mother conceived me." According to Doctors Minirth and Meier, well-known Christian psychiatrists and authors, man is not basically good as Rogers believed. The Bible claims that no human is sinless and that man can never satisfy God by attempting to establish his own righteousness (Romans 7: 14-25; 10: 1-4).[101]

If our world view originates from the premise that man has a sinful nature, we then have a point of reference (God's truth) on which to build. Building a school of thought, whether it is in the area of philosophy, psychology, or science, has a better chance of staying on track when the reference point is divine rather than human.

According to the French philosopher Blaise Pascal (1623-1662), every man has a "God-shaped vacuum" inside. People innately search for meaning in their life. "According to logotherapy, the striving to find a meaning in one's life is the primary motivational force in man. That is why I speak of a will to meaning in contrast to the pleasure principle (or, as we could also term it, the will to pleasure)."[102]

In psychotherapy man needs to be understood in three dimensions: body, soul, and spirit. It is of vital importance to understand man in a holistic way. He is a physical, psychological, and spiritual being. All three of these dimensions are interrelated.[103] The problem with some of the schools of psychology is that they address the physical and the psychological but ignore the spiritual side. "If the counselor is going to be of any practical help to his clients, he must begin with a thorough knowledge of the nature of man. Fundamental to understanding the nature of man is the realization that man without Christ is lost. To ignore a counselee's eternal destiny while helping him solve his present problems is utterly illogical."[104]

The sinful nature of man and the importance of understanding this cannot be overemphasized. This means that man is flawed and to use himself as a reference point in understanding the meaning of life is ridiculous.

According to Viktor Frankl, a psychiatrist who developed "logotherapy," "Logos is a Greek word that denotes meaning!"[105] From a Biblical-Christian viewpoint, we could apply this to John 1:1 and 1:14. "In the beginning was the Word [meaning], and the Word [meaning] was with God, and the Word [meaning] was God." (John 1:1 NASB). "And the Word [meaning] became flesh, and dwelt among us . . ." (John 1:14 NASB).

We now have two reference points. The first is understanding that the basic nature of man is sinful. The second is that through

Chart 5
Four Types Of Therapy *

	Insight-oriented	Behavior-oriented	Experiential-oriented	Christian
Representative Schools	1. Psychoanalysis (Freud) 2. Analytical psychology (Jung) 3. Individual psychology (Adler) 4. Psychoanalytic psychotherapy (Fromm, Reichmann) 5. Short-term psychotherapy (Sifneos, Malan) 6. Hypnoanalysis (Wolberg) 7. Brief or emergency psychotherapy	1. Reciprocal inhibition or behavior therapy (Wolpe) 2. Modeling therapy (Bandura) 3. Directive psychology (Thorne) 4. Behavior modification (for use with inpatients) 5. Rational-emotive therapy (Ellis) 6. Reality therapy (Glasser) 7. Transactional analysis (Berne) 8. Biofeedback (Green)	1. Client-centered (Rogers) 2. Gestalt (Perls) 3. Primal scream (Janov) 4. Logotherapy (Frankl) 5. Reparenting	1. Psychology more important than Scripture 2. Psychology parallel with Scripture 3. Scripture opposed to psychology 4. Scripture integrated with psychology 5. Scripture integrated with but regarded as more in than psychology
Basic Divisions	A continuum from short-term to psychoanalysis	1. Earlier schools—emphasis on over fears and behavior 2. More recent schools—emphasis on beliefs (Ellis) 3. Majority of most-recent schools—emphasis on biofeedback	1. Philosophic (Rogers) 2. Somatic	See above
Mental Disorders Treated	Neuroses, personality disorders	Some neuroses, psychoses	Low self-image	All
Concept of Pathology	Unconscious conflicts	Inappropriate learned behavior	Loss of human potential	Physical, psychological, and spiritual difficulties (holistic view)
Goal of Treatment	Conflict resolution	Removal of inappropriate behavior	Actualization of potential	Health of the whole man, especially spiritual maturity

Mode of Attaining Goal	In-depth insight	Direct learning	Immediate experiencing	Eclectic approach—depending on the needs of the individual
Time Focus	Past	Objective present	The moment	Past-present-future
Type of Treatment	Long-term, intense	Short-term, not intense	Short-term, intense	Length and intensity vary
Counselor's Task	To comprehend unconscious	To shape behavior	To express himself openly	To understand and treat the problems of the whole man
Counselor's Role	Indirect—to reflect and interrupt	Direct and practical—to advise	To accept the counselee without condition	To determine and utilize an approach suitable to the particular situation (see I Thess 5:14)
Techniques	Free association, transference	Conditioning	A variety including verbal and somatic methods	Use of Scripture and scientific methods
Treatment Model	Doctor-patient (therapeutic alliance)	Teacher-student (learning alliance)	Peer-peer (human alliance)	Shepherd-member of flock (spiritual alliance)
Nature of Relationship	Artificial relationship for the purpose of finding a cure	Genuine, but for the sake of finding a cure	Genuine, but primarily to find a cure	Genuine relationship which is used in the search for a cure
Crucial Point Ignored by the General Theory	Insight alone may not result in change	Man is more than a computer	Man is not all good	

* Frank Minirth, M.D. and Paul Meier, M.D., *Counseling and the Nature of Man* (Grand Rapids, Michigan: Baker Book House, 1982), P. 54-55. Used by permission of Drs. Minirth and Meier. Drs. Minirth and Meier based most of this chart on Toksoz B. Karaus, "Psychotherapies: An Overview," *American Journal of Psychiatry* 134:8 (1977): 851-63. The characterization of Christian counseling is based in part on John D. Carter, "Secular and Sacred Models of Psychology and Religion," *Journal of Psychology and Theology* (1977): 197-208, and in part on the ideas and experience of Drs. Minirth and Meier.

Jesus Christ we have meaning and purpose in life. Apart from Jesus Christ we are lost. Jesus said ". . . I am the way, and the truth, and the life; no one comes to the Father, but through Me" (John 14:6 NASB).

Chart 5 compares four psychotherapies in an overview format. The fourth form of therapy is Christian – eclectic. It is superior to the other types but employs and integrates them where it is useful. It considers God's relationship to man, which is not considered in the other three categories.

TWO KINGDOMS / TWO FOUNDATIONS

We have discussed man's thinking process as expressed through philosophers, psychologists, and scientists. The reason for this extended discussion on man's world view is to understand where it originates.

"In eternity past there was only one will, the will of God. There was no evil whatsoever, only harmony, holiness, and righteousness. When the second will entered the universe, generated by the heart of Lucifer, rebellion broke out. Time, as we know it, began with two wills in existence."[106]

Lucifer, otherwise known as Satan, is an extremely powerful force in rebellion against God. He has also led man into rebellion, starting with Adam and Eve.

One of Satan's strategies is to influence the mind. When Satan controls man's thought process and world view, he gains control of the person and impacts the lives of others. Satan's aim is to control man's thoughts, promote a lie, and oppose God's truth. Once a person's thoughts are controlled, Satan can control that person's behavior.[107] A few Biblical examples of Satan putting thoughts into a person's mind include: David (I Chronicles 21:1); Judas (John 13:2); and Ananias (Acts 5:3).

Satan deceives each individual to believe that all of his thoughts are his own. In many (probably most) cases, the unbeliever does not believe in Satan. He, therefore, believes he is the originator of his thoughts as in the examples of the previously mentioned philosophers. For believers in Jesus Christ, the Bible sheds light on our struggles that appear to be human conflict. "For our struggle is not against flesh and blood, but against the rulers, against the powers, against the world forces of this darkness, against the spiritual forces of wickedness in the heavenly places" (Ephesians 6:12 NASB). Satan works undercover and is a liar. In reference to Satan, Jesus said, ". . . He was a murderer from the beginning, and does not stand in the truth, because there is no truth in him. Whenever he speaks a lie, he speaks from his own nature, for he is a liar and the father of lies" (John 8:44 NASB).

Satan lies to us and influences our thoughts. "Satan is the ruler of this world and the whole world is in his power (John 12:31; I John 5:19)."[108] When Adam and Eve sinned, they gave up their authority and rulership over God's creation.

Neil Anderson describes the transfer of authority and rulership in his book, *Bondage Breaker*. Using the Bible as his source, he makes the following three points:
1. We were all born spiritually dead and subject to Satan or "the prince of the power of the air" (Ephesians 2:2).
2. When we accept Christ as our Savior, we are transferred from the kingdom of darkness to the kingdom of God's Son (Colossians 1:13).
3. Our citizenship was transferred from earth to heaven (Philippians 3:20), and from Satan to Christ as our ruler.[109]

Satan is the ruler of this world but he has limitations in accordance with God's will. He can do nothing without God's permission (Job 1:6-12). God actively restrains Satan (Job 1:12; 2:6).

Satan has a hierarchy of fallen angels who work to carry out his purpose. We see this in Ephesians 6:12, quoted above. A specific example of this is seen in Daniel 10:12-13, where an angel was sent to deliver a message to Daniel. The angel Gabriel tells Daniel about an encounter with the prince of the kingdom of

Persia (fallen angel). Michael (good angel, see Jude 1:9) helps Gabriel, who says: " . . . and I have come in response to your words. But the prince of the kingdom of Persia was withstanding me for twenty-one days; then behold, Michael, one of the chief princes, came to help me, for I had been left there with the kings of Persia" (Daniel 10:12-13 NASB).

There are two errors in belief concerning Satan. One is a disbelief in him. Mankind can deny his existence and believe there is only one supernatural power in the universe. This is in harmony with many New Age beliefs. The other error is to have an unhealthy interest in the demonic, elevating Satan as an equal with God. Satan would love man to believe either error. They are both lies.

Satan attacks mankind in two different ways. Minirth and Meier describe Satan's tactics as a two-prong attack. He desires to keep the nonbeliever in spiritual darkness (John 3:19-21). Secondly, he wants to destroy the mental health of Christians (Ephesians 6: 11-16; I Peter 8: 8-9). Satan does this through deceiving people to believe in false beliefs (I Timothy 4: 1-3). He can influence our thinking (Matthew 16: 21-23) and hinder the spread of the gospel (I Thessalonians 2:2, 14-16).[110]

Mankind has a choice of one of two foundations he can build on. According to the gospel of Matthew, Jesus says, "Therefore, everyone who hears these words of Mine, and acts upon them, may be compared to a wise man, who built his house upon the rock; and the rain descended, and the floods came, and the winds blew, and burst against that house; and yet it did not fall; for it had been founded upon the rock" (Matthew 7:24-25 NASB). What we believe is extremely important. If we build a belief system on the Word of God, we have a guide for this present life as well as eternity.

In regard to the second foundation, Jesus says, "and every one who hears these words of Mine, and does not act upon them, will be like a foolish man, who built his house upon the sand, and the rain descended, and the floods came, and the winds blew, and burst against that house; and it fell, and great was its fall" (Matthew 7:26-27 NASB). Mankind's alternative is to ignore God's Word and build a belief system on what the philosophers had to say using themselves as a reference point.

We are faced with a choice of reference points to discern truth. Do we choose God's way or Satan's way (usually disguised as man's way)? Do we have an external thermometer based on God's truth or an internal thermometer based on our own subjective nature?

WHERE IS YOUR THERMOMETER?

According to the American Heritage Dictionary of the English Language, cold blooded in a zoological sense is "having a bodily temperature that varies with the external environment." In other words, a cold-blooded animal's body (such as a lobster) conforms to the external temperature. You can slowly increase the temperature of the water until it boils and the lobster boils (or dies). The cold-blooded animal cannot determine the temperature until it is too late.

In the same manner, a person who determines truth or establishes a world view based on his own subjective nature is like the man who builds his house on the sand. The thermometer inside himself rises and falls with the culture and opinions of other people. According to the New Age movement, there is no one right religion. Every person defines his own truth.[111]

If truth is defined by the individual, and each person has a different truth, what is truth? In the Gospel of John, when Jesus was being tried before Pilate, He said, "' . . . I have come into the world to bear witness to the truth. Every one who is of the truth hears My voice.' Pilate said to Him, 'What is truth?'" (John 18:37-38 NASB). From Pilate's frame of reference, himself, he came to the only conclusion possible.

Having an internal thermometer (standard) or subjective measurement of truth is essentially the philosophy of humanism.

Humanism is a system that puts man in the center. He begins with himself and tries to rationally build a belief system to find knowledge, meaning, and value. He uses himself as his integration point.[112]

It is impossible for a man to determine truth and meaning in life when left to his own reasoning ability. Man's basic nature is flawed by sin, which distorts his ability to reason apart from God's truth. According to the Book of Proverbs, we are directed to "trust in the Lord with all your heart, and do not lean on your own understanding. In all your ways acknowledge Him, and He will make your paths straight" (Proverbs 3:5-6 NASB).

God tells us in His Word not to trust our own reasoning apart from Him. If we choose to take the humanist approach, it will lead to death. "There is a way which seems right to a man, but its end is the way of death."[113]

If we rely on an external thermometer (standard outside of self) we have a standard independent of our sinful nature and subjectivity. In contrast to our earlier analogy of a cold-blooded animal, we now have a warm-blooded animal. A warm-blooded animal cannot be slowly boiled in a physical sense, without its awareness.

Mankind (warm-blooded creatures) can be boiled mentally and have their conscience desensitized slowly yet completely, and without their awareness. Even the true believers who have a relationship with Christ can become desensitized to immoral behavior when they get away from God's Word.

Man's external thermometer consists of a standard outside of man himself. It is God's truth as revealed in the Bible. God's standard is an objective standard.

As we mentioned earlier, Satan is the god of this world but is bound by the limitations God imposes on him. He works through our culture and media to deceive and turn mankind away from God. "Not only is man lost, incomplete, and depraved, but he is under constant attack by a most powerful enemy – Satan. Satan is more powerful, clever, and shrewd than most people realize."[114]

Our culture and media, for the most part, are determined by human beings with a basic sin nature who are heavily influenced by Satan. The culture and media influences the population at large. It is a downward cyclical spiral that feeds on itself. Remember Proverbs 14:12, which says, "There is a way that seems right to a man, but its end is the way of death."

Satan's influence + man's sinful nature → influences media → distorts reality for the mass population → forms our culture → influences our world view (belief system).

Concerning the New Age movement, Missler and Eastman state: "the prophets of the New Age claim that we are rapidly headed for a new understanding of our place in the universe and that sin, the notion that we have missed the mark in the eyes of God, is an archaic belief which will have no place in the coming new age."[115] We are in this New Age presently. To mention the Judeo-Christian world view of the concept of "sin" is considered archaic and primitive.

CONTRASTING WORLD VIEWS / BELIEF SYSTEMS

God's Way

- Foundation is the Bible (II Timothy 3:16)
- Man's nature is sinful (Psalm 51:5; Romans 7:14-25)
- Salvation through a relationship with Jesus Christ alone (John 14:6)
- Results are: love, joy, peace, patience, kindness, goodness, faithfulness, gentleness, and self control (Galatians 5:22-23), eternal salvation (John 3:16; Romans 6:23)

Satan's Way

- Based on man's thinking apart from God (Proverbs 14:12; Psalm 14:1)

- Man's nature is good or neutral (Philosophers, psychologists, scientists)
- Salvation through many different ways or religions (Matthew 7:13)
- Results are immorality, impurity, sensuality, idolatry, sorcery, enmities, strife, jealousy, outbursts of anger, disputes, dissensions, factions, envying, drunkenness, carousing (Galatians 5:19-21), and eternal damnation (Matthew 25:41, 46; Luke 16:23-31; Revelation 20:15).

We have covered two world views, two kingdoms, and two foundations. Reality is a world view that is dualistic. This dualism is not one of equality. It consists of good and evil, God and Satan, but they are not equal opposites. God is the Creator. Satan was originally created as a good angel named Lucifer. He was a beautiful, powerful angel who rebelled against God his Creator (Ezekiel 28:14-17).

To understand prophecy, we must comprehend the importance of our world view and the foundation of that view. What roles do faith and reason play in the development of our world view?

FAITH AND REASON

Faith and reason sound like contradictory terms. The word "faith" often implies stupidity or ignorance. Sometimes in theology it may mean faith in faith itself. "Probably the best way to describe this concept of modern theology is to say that it is faith in faith, rather than faith directed to an object which is actually there."[116] For Christianity the value of faith is directed upon an object. It is not a subjective mystical experience.

True Christian faith should not be based on an existential experience as the philosopher Kierkegaard suggests. As previously discussed, he believes we find truth through a "leap of faith." Reason is disregarded.

The Christian faith is built on historical facts. There is sufficient evidence to believe in Biblical revelation as discussed earlier.

Francis Schaeffer equates the word "grace" with faith, and the word "nature" with rational ability or reason. If we presuppose that the humanist (using himself as a point of reference) seeks truth in a rational way, he will be led to meaninglessness and despair (nature's outcome). The non-rational approach (grace) leads to meaning.

According to Schaeffer, this tension between nature (reason) and grace (faith) was to find a meaning for the two together. Philosophers have tried to unite the two based on reason. The answer to solving this struggle can only be found in the "full Biblical system." It is because these philosophers have looked for a rationalistic and humanistic answer that they failed.[117]

Reason alone, from a human reference point, cannot help man to find real meaning and purpose in life but only despair. Schaeffer's "line of despair" started with Hegel when he threw out absolutes and the need for a Creator. Kierkegaard threw out reason for experience or a "leap of faith."

These men struggled to blend faith and reason to find meaning in life. Coming from a self-reference or humanistic viewpoint in their thinking, they had to sacrifice one to save the other.

The Bible teaches both concepts. Proverbs 3:5 says, "Trust in the Lord with all your heart, and do not lean on your own understanding." This, along with many other Scriptures, says "faith" is the answer, not reason. Isaiah 1:18 says, "Come now, and let us reason together; says the Lord." Here the Scripture says reason is important. Consider the following statement from the manual used in a well-known 12 step program.

> We couldn't duck the issue. Some of us had already walked over the Bridge of Reason toward the desired shore of faith. The outlines and the promise of the New Land had brought luster to tired eyes and fresh courage to flagging spirits. Friendly hands had stretched out in welcome. We were grateful that reason had brought us

> so far. But somehow we couldn't quite step ashore . . . without knowing it, had we not been brought to where we stood by a certain kind of faith?[118]

Using reason, based on God's Word, as our reference point, we can begin our study of the defense of the Christian faith. We have discussed some of the evidence in previous chapters, including prophecy. The problem is that reason alone will not lead us by itself all the way to truth and salvation. God requires faith.

INFINITE (faith)

_____   Man can only cross this line **by faith built on reason - -**

FINITE (reason)

God comes to our level through Biblical revelation to reason with us. Based on this Biblical revelation, we take a step of faith and meet God at the Cross of Jesus Christ. God allows us to connect with the infinite (Himself) but does not allow us to understand His thoughts or His ways. Isaiah 55:8-9 says, "'For My thoughts are not your thoughts, neither are your ways My ways,' declares the Lord. 'For as the heavens are higher than the earth, so are My ways higher than your ways, and My thoughts than your thoughts.'" This is the tension point; we reach God through faith built on reason and historical evidence. He reaches us through His Word and His Son Jesus Christ.

REASON + FAITH → Confirms Reliability of Bible → Reveals TRUTH and SALVATION

A recurring theme throughout this chapter has been man's erroneous reasoning process when his reference point is centered in himself. Man's sinful nature is the underlying reason humanism does not work. Man's reasoning process from a humanistic perspective is contrasted with a reasoning process using God's Word as a reference point. The chapter concluded with a discussion of faith and reason.

As we add the third level to our pyramid, we are introduced to our next chapter, "Signs of the Times." We will see what happens when human technology surpasses man's morality and spiritual connection with his Creator.

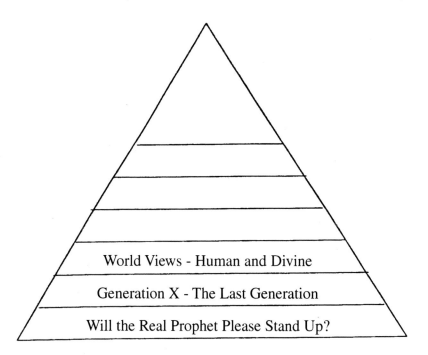

- FOUR -

SIGNS OF THE TIMES

"Even so you too, when you see these things happening, recognize that He is near, right at the door."
Mark 13:29 NASB

In the previous chapter, we reviewed world views and how, apart from God's Word, man's reasoning process leads to an erroneous conclusion because of his basic sin nature. We saw how the ultimate spiritual battle is the battle for the mind.

Chapter Four shows the results of increased knowledge and technology in the hands of mankind apart from God. We will see how this combination lays the groundwork for a one world government.

KNOWLEDGE EXPLOSION

"But as for you, Daniel, conceal these words and seal up the book until the end of time; many will go back and forth, and knowledge will increase" (Daniel 12:4).

Human knowledge has been on the increase since the beginning of mankind. How does Daniel's prophecy about the increase in knowledge apply to our day and time? This prophecy could be plugged into any point in history.

The answer lies in the rate of the increase. According to most experts, the sum total of all human knowledge doubles every two years.[119]

When we consider the history of mankind and the vast knowledge that has accumulated, this rate of accumulation is nothing short of phenomenal. Peter and Paul Lalonde, in their book *2000 A.D.*, discuss the rate of accumulation of knowledge over the last 6000 years. It would look like Chart 6. Each time frame is shorter. The rate in this generation is exponential. The rate of doubling is now believed to be less than two years.[120]

This exponential increase in knowledge takes on prophetic significance in light of Daniel 12:9. "And he said, 'go your way, Daniel, for these words are concealed and sealed up until the end time.'" Daniel could not understand the prophetic visions that were given to him (Daniel 12:8). The key to understanding Daniel's prophecy is the tremendous increase in knowledge that is present in the "end times." Prophecy can be understood in light of current events and the exponential increase in knowledge. Prophecy, like a puzzle, begins to portray the real picture.

Peter and Paul Lalonde, in their book *2000 A.D.*, give an excellent example of exponential growth. If you are paid an income for one month starting with one penny on day one and double your amount each day, by mid-month or day 15 your total is $327.67. By day 25 your total is $335,544.31. Now the amount of money you have accumulated is a big deal. By day 31 the total is $21,474,836.47. Exponential growth has taken on a new meaning.[121]

It is those last days of the month that are significant, especially the last three days. Knowledge increase has demonstrated a similar growth. If you look at the following chart, we are in that time zone where the charted line is almost vertical. To use the money example, **we are in the last three days of the month**.

Real Generation Gap

A generation gap historically would explain the reason why parents and children did not understand each other. The music was

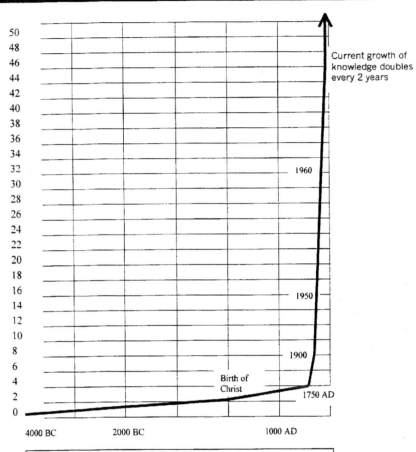

Chart 6

different along with different hairstyles and clothing styles. The two generations just did not talk the same language.

With the exponential growth in both knowledge and technology, this gap has widened considerably. "The technology explosion has created the first true generation gap in human history. In the past kids wore their hair differently from their parents or listened to different music. But today they truly live in a different world. They're plugged in, they're on-line, and they view the world through a lens that the older generation doesn't even know exists."[122]

The first true generation gap makes sense, considering the rebirth of Israel as a nation on May 14, 1948, and considering the words of Jesus, "truly, I say to you, this generation will not pass away until all these things take place" (Matthew 24: 34 NASB). If we are living in the last generation, as many believe, the exponential increase in *knowledge and technology* would take place during this generation. Remember that knowledge was doubling every two years in 1997. In the year 2000, this rate has again increased.

Internet – Knowledge Communication Explosion

The internet was designed by Larry Roberts in the early 1960's. Lalonde traces the development of the internet. The internet was originally called Arpanet, and came into existence as a result of the cold war. The military commissioned the government to create a communication system that would continue to function in the event of a nuclear attack. Messages were delivered in packets of information that could take alternate paths to reach a destination. As a result, the internet was born.[123]

Since the internet "piggybacks" our present telephone system, it was easy to cover the entire world in a short period of time. This technological leap caused a quantum leap in communication in the information age. Remember Daniel 12:4, ". . . many will go back and forth and knowledge will increase."

We truly have a global communication network in place. Since the internet was essentially dependent on telephone lines, it was not possible to connect the whole world with the internet. Today it is becoming possible to connect the entire world electronically, due to advances in satellite and cellular phone technologies.[124]

We are now in the process of a wireless revolution. In 1999, a *Time* magazine advertisement for Agilent Technologies, illustrates the explosion of a global communication network. The ad states, "It took one hundred years to connect the first billion people. The second will take only five. The wireless revolution is at hand."[125]

Babel Revisited

In Genesis 11, mankind initially disobeyed God's commandment to scatter over the earth. Prior to their disobedience, ". . . the whole earth used the same language and the same words" (Genesis 11:1 NASB).

As a direct result of their disobedience, God confused their language and they scattered over the "face of the whole earth" (Genesis 11:7-9 NASB). The city and tower they built was then named "Babel" or Babylon, which means to confuse.

According to biblical prophecy, the world will come under the rule of the revived Roman Empire and the Antichrist (Daniel 2:40-43; 7:7-8; Revelation 13:4-18). The need for efficient communication in the same language would lay the groundwork for this future prophecy to be fulfilled.

Computer software translates web pages and other material into many different languages, including English, German, Spanish and French in less than twenty seconds.[126] One of the most substantial barriers to a united world (multiple languages) is now removed. The stage is rapidly being set for a worldwide government under the authority of the Antichrist, by the increase in technology and knowledge, and the ability to communicate quickly and efficiently on a global basis.

Thus, combining Daniel 12:4 and Daniel 12:8-9 shows prophecy in a new light.

"'But you, Daniel, shut up the words, and seal the book until the time of the end [before the Second Coming of Christ]; many shall run to and fro [ease of travel], and knowledge shall increase.' ...Although I heard, I did not understand. 'My Lord what shall be the end of these things?' [Explain it to me]. And he said 'Go your way, Daniel, for the words are closed up and sealed till the time of the end'" [Go about your business. This prophecy will not be understood until the last days] (Daniel 12:4, 8, 9 NKJV). The exponential growth of knowledge and technology, coupled with being part of the last generation, gives us insight into Daniel's prophecy that would not have been possible 100 years ago.

THE QUICKENING

A number of people are beginning to realize that something is about to happen. Perhaps as the rate of acceleration increases, there is a sense of a judgment or a major event just on the horizon.

"In 1995, Art Bell, a late night radio talk show host, coined a term to describe the accelerating pace of events in the last few years. He called it 'The Quickening.'" [127] Bell, in his book, *The Art of Talk*, claims he has witnessed an acceleration of events in every aspect of human life. He has seen the escalation of violence, rebellion against authority and blatant looting. He has also seen the acceleration of dramatically changing weather patterns, including an increase in earthquakes, hurricanes and other acts of nature.[128]

The term "quickening" describes the first move of the fetus inside the womb. Art Bell uses this term to describe the time leading up to a climactic event. Ironically, Jesus also used similar terms such as pregnancy, labor, and childbirth as they relate to the signs preceding the Second Coming. For example, in Matthew, He says, "For nation will rise against nation, and kingdom against kingdom, and in various places there will be famines and earthquakes. But these things are merely the beginning of birth pangs" (Matthew 24:7-8 NASB).

The quickening is the start of movement by the fetus, which precedes false labor, real labor, and then birth. Prophetically speaking, the quickening would parallel the accelerated pace of events (signs preceding the Second Coming). The actual labor pains would parallel world judgment (the tribulation period). The false labor pains (between the quickening and actual labor) are very likely where humanity is at the present time.

Today all the signs of the Second Coming are happening at an accelerated rate. The only event that lies between today and the tribulation period (labor pains), is the rapture of the church, which will be discussed in a later chapter.

Given all the current events and biblical prophecies, scoffers in the last days will misinterpret signs of the Lord's return. The Apostle Peter said, "Know this first of all, that in the last days mockers will come with their mocking, following after their own lusts, and saying, 'Where is the promise of His coming?' For ever since the fathers fell asleep, all continues just as it was from the beginning of creation" (II Peter 3:3-4 NASB).

Childbirth and the Second Coming of Jesus are both preceded by well-known signs in advance of the actual event. An ill-prepared mother, like the skeptic, can ignore the signs and be caught unaware when the child is born.[129]

". . . The day of the Lord will come just like a thief in the night. While they are saying 'Peace and safety!' then destruction will come upon them suddenly like birth pangs upon a woman with child; and they shall not escape" (I Thessalonians 5:2-3 NASB). The "day of the Lord" in Scripture, often, and definitely in this case, refers to a day of judgment.

This reference in Thessalonians describes the suddenness in which the worldwide tribulation period will begin. If you want to accept Jesus Christ as your Lord and Savior, Who paid the penalty for your sins, ask Him in prayer to come into your life and save you. He promises to respond to you. Revelation 3:20 says, "Behold, I stand at the door and knock; if any one hears My voice and opens the door, I will come in to him, and will dine with him and he with Me." The choice is yours; choose Him before the "day of the Lord" comes.

ENVIRONMENTAL MANIPULATION – WHO IS IN CONTROL?

Does our environment control our thoughts and behavior as psychologist B. F. Skinner believes? If he is correct, one must be very cautious about who or what controls our environment.

The U.S. Army conducted a study of World War II combat veterans. Through private, confidential interviews, they found that only 15 to 20% of the soldiers fired their weapons in a combat situation. The vast majority of the killing was done by less than 5% of the soldiers.[130]

The military became very concerned over this problem. One of their approaches to manipulate the environment was to change target practice patterns. "One of the approaches that they tried (with tremendous success) was to replace the paper bulls-eye targets used during shooting practice with more realistic looking human pop-up targets. The results were staggering. During the Vietnam War, 95 percent of soldiers were firing their weapons in battle."[131]

It is well known that more psychological problems exist among Vietnam Vets than previous war veterans. This change in percentage of soldiers firing weapons may have been a contributing factor. Environmental manipulation changed behavior.

In this example, environmental manipulation desensitized their conscience. "Systematic desensitization" is a well-known behavioral technique for treating certain psychological problems. In this case, the "problem" was their sensitive conscience. The treatment or solution was to desensitize the soldier's conscience or teach him to act contrary to his morals.

Passive behavior which involves fantasy violence or immorality through television, movies, or books can also desensitize a person's conscience. Virtual reality (VR) is as close as one can get to the real thing through a fantasy interaction. "Virtual reality technology refers to computer technology that allows you to move through and interact with a three dimensional, computer generated environment."[132]

The implications of computer technology, the internet, virtual reality, and video games are astounding. On the positive side, modern day computer technology can be used to train surgeons without actually doing surgery and pilots without actually flying. It can also be used to treat psychological problems such as phobias.

Unfortunately, the same technology can use violence and pornography to desensitize man's conscience and soul. Desensitization has been utilized in a negative way. It becomes much easier to engage in a violent or immoral act for the first time in the real world, after it has been repeatedly committed in a fantasy world. In VR, the experience is in a safe world before taken outside to the real world for the ultimate thrill.[133]

One World Culture

People around the world are learning English through the media. They are watching American movies and CNN. In addition to learning English, they are learning Hollywood's cultural values, which are understood as American values.[134]

The spread of cultural values worldwide, especially through the media, has a unifying worldwide effect. In a short period of time, a worldwide cultural value system will incorporate a unity of mind, thought and beliefs. Through the use of media and computer technology, these values will become widespread. "Like UFO's and VR, artificial intelligence has the ability to get human kind to accept a totally new view of reality, life, our origins, and our future. Isn't it amazing that once again it's all happening in the very generation that saw Israel return to her land – the very generation in which the Bible said that humankind would be led into global confusion and deception."[135]

This union of a new mindset and world view will be based on the power of the occult. This will be the first united culture since the Tower of Babel. A global culture is being restored; it is not one of God our Creator, but is of the "god of this world." It is united by the same god behind the original Tower of Babel.

Control the Media / Control the World

"Whoever controls the media – the images - controls the culture." Allen Ginsberg

Think of the power and influence of one man with absolute control over the media. He would have the ability to report the news selectively, thus distorting the news. He could do editorials of his choosing. He could distort images on the screen to portray an illusion of reality. Ultimately, he could create the world view he wanted you to believe. Sound outrageous? The process has already begun.

Many television watchers are losing the ability to discern reality when the producer's intent is not malicious. Today's television audience has trouble separating reality from fantasy. According to a *Times Mirror* poll, 50% of those who watched reality shows such as *Cops* or *Rescue 911* believed they were watching it live (the real thing), even though the bottom of the screen stated it was a re-enactment.[136]

The world today is very much a created world. It is created by the media upon our culture. The line between reality and delusion is becoming increasingly blurred. If the news isn't reported accurately, and if movies portray an artificial, created value system as "normal" and acceptable, how do we know the truth?

"'The mass media can covertly modify public perception,' according to Bonnie Reiss, a former Hollywood attorney and environmental activist. She said, 'There are a few thousand people who could affect a few million.'"[137]

In the following sections, we will see the power of the media. It becomes increasingly difficult to separate reality from deception.

Visibility of the Media Industry

This has become one of the largest, yet most secretive industries. The industry creates characters using everything from cosmetic surgery to lessons in public speaking.

They can take a politician or celebrity and change their image (looks, body language, speech, etc.) to suit their purposes. It can literally create the celebrities it chooses.

It is important that the media industry remains secretive. According to Lalonde, it must remain secretive or hidden or their clients would be seen as created images instead of something special. The celebrity creators produce powerful images, thus creating a commodity for a market. The celebrity then uses this created position to voice opinions.[138]

The industry creates a celebrity who isn't real. The celebrity, who doesn't exist as portrayed, then influences the masses.

Is something wrong with this picture? An industry creates someone who doesn't exist (but the masses think they do exist), who has the power to influence a vast population. If insanity is a break from reality, then this is it.

Digital Media Deception

Digital technology can be used to manipulate images or people to appear in a different place or a different context. It has been used in movies to portray celebrities or presidents in a context to fit into the movie's plot.

The problem, like any other advance in technology, is that it can be used to distort reality such as news stories. For example,

CBS made a decision on New Year's Eve 1999, (12/31/99), to cover up a giant NBC-sponsored screen that appeared behind Dan Rather in Times Square. They digitally superimposed the CBS logo over the NBC sign.

"'This may seem like an innocent little corporate coup, but there are bigger implications in terms of eroding people's confidence in what they see on the screen' said Richard Kaplar, vice president of the Media Institute, a communications think tank in Washington."[139]

Digital technology has the potential for disaster by manipulating the masses to distort reality. Another example of this deception is the following possible news release as quoted from *2000 A.D.*

> (AP) Baghdad - Saddam Hussein . . . was removed from power today. Hussein was overthrown by a popular uprising sparked by footage of him drinking alcohol and eating pork. . . . [I]t has been learned that the footage of Hussein drinking alcohol and eating pork had actually been digitally created and fed to Iraqi television by the CIA.[140] [Not reality].

Most of what we know about the world today comes from the media. The potential for fraud and media manipulation is in place and will very likely be used during the Tribulation Period to support the Antichrist as the world ruler.

Reporting the News or Creating the News?

A person comes home from work and turns on the TV to watch the six o'clock news. Or a person picks up his local newspaper to catch up on the world news. No problem! Right? Not necessarily.

Most people believe the news that is reported. However, it is not necessarily 100% accurate. In reality, the media chooses the news that is reported. The media chooses how and if an event will be reported. Unfortunately, the mass population does not have an objective, unbiased report of what is really going on in the world.

The power of the news media is unparalleled. It tells you what and who to believe. Ted Turner once claimed that his CNN network brought down the Berlin Wall. This type of statement is typical for Ted Turner. Nonetheless, the people who define our mental boundaries today establish tomorrow's economic, political, and military boundaries.[141]

Not only does the news media influence the beliefs and behavior of the masses, it also influences our policy makers. For example, "When CNN floods the airwaves with a particular news story, politicians have virtually no choice but to redirect their attention to the crisis that CNN has chosen for them. Many worry that this has made CNN the sixth vote on the United Nations Security Council."[142]

We have discussed how philosophers, psychologists, and scientists have influenced our belief system; the news media also has an ongoing influence over our belief system. Television has become our window to the world. It tells us what to believe, what to expect and what to shun. Instead of seeing the world as it is, TV bends and shapes the world into the form the producer chooses.[143]

The influence of the media combined with the ability to transmit information quickly (internet), sets the world stage for the fulfillment of prophecy. No generation besides ours has had a way to transmit information effectively so prophecy could be fulfilled. The media is an integral part of the groundwork.

John tells us in Revelation 13 that the Antichrist (also known as the beast) will have "'a mouth speaking great things' and that he will become the leader of 'all kindred, and tongues, and nations.' That all the world will be mesmerized by the beast. And also that 'all that dwell upon the earth shall worship him' (vv. 5, 7, 8). Once again, how could the entire world have even heard of this guy, let alone turn the reigns of the world over to him, without the power of today's global television systems?"[144]

As we mentioned earlier, the media has tremendous potential. A person's name, unknown by the general population, can become a household word overnight. This happened early in the year 2000 with media attention focused on Elian, the Cuban boy rescued from the sea after his mother died attempting to flee from Cuba. This media exposure is exactly what the coming Antichrist will need to gain power, influence, and authority rapidly.

ONE WORLD – GLOBAL CONTROL

One world government? Sounds like the answer to man's problems. How is it possible? There have always been "wars and rumors of wars" (Matthew 24:6 NASB). When there isn't war between nations, there are civil and ethnic wars within nations.

Is it possible that the world will be united and at peace? There is good news and bad news. The good news is that there will be peace for a short period of time and the bad news is that it will end abruptly (I Thessalonians 5:3).

The world is moving rapidly toward a one-world government. "Back in 1918, Russian Communist Leon Trotsky wrote in *Bolshevism and World Peace*: 'the task of the proletariat is to create a United States of Europe, as the foundation for the United States of the World.'"[145] There is clearly a movement in that direction. We had the European Common Market, the European Economic Community and the European Union.

World government is not just a possibility, it is a prophetic reality. The United Nations Commission on Global Governance did a three-year study on how to implement world government by the year 2000.[146]

Our worldwide communication system is in place; a world government could become a reality in the near future. This may not occur this year but has a high probability for the near future.

The Council of Foreign Relations (CFR) was founded in 1921. It was the prime mover for the establishment of the United Nations in 1945. More recently, the Club of Rome Conference, composed of elite leaders of the world, suggested a move toward world government by dividing the world into ten regions, each with an appointed head, with representation at the U.N.[147]

Environmental Concerns or a Hidden Agenda

Environmental and social concerns will be vehicles that are used by the U.N. to consolidate its power. A plan to restructure the U.N. Trusteeship Council would give 23 individuals extraordinary international powers over the "global commons."[148] The "global commons" deal with everything related to our environment and how it contributes to the support of human life.

This intense environmental concern has some New Age and pagan overtones. Millions of acres of national parkland in Utah have been considered off limits to tourism; they were designated a wilderness in 1997 under President Clinton. "All this is merely part of the U.N.'s bigger picture – Agenda 21; a blueprint for global environmental dictatorship that calls for 're-wilding' at least half the continental United States. The premise of the whole program is that human society is a cancer on the planet and that radical surgery is required to bring it under control."[149]

In other words, our planet needs to be purged. This hints of paganism and nature worship. There is a new and growing trend toward this old religion. It's a combination of nature worship, mysticism, and paganism. If you don't believe this, research paganism through the internet. What used to be considered an ancient religion in the Old Testament days is now a contemporary religion.

Maurice Strong, a millionaire, is a "pillar" of the Temple of Understanding, and secretary general of the first U.N. Earth Summit. He built a Babylonian sun god temple on his ranch in Colorado, which serves as a center of New Age religious activities.[150] We are entering an age where the ancient Babylonian religion and paganism will again unify the world.

A one-world government and a one-world religion may look appealing from a human perspective, but not from a divine perspective. United Nations Assistant Secretary General Robert Muller once wrote: "'If Christ came back to earth, his first visit would be to the United Nations to see if his dream of human oneness and brotherhood had come true.' Muller, by the way is associated with the Lucis Trust, a New Age organization that evolved from the Lucis publishing company, previously known as the Lucifer Publishing Company. Draw your own conclusions about which master such men serve."[151]

The Money Connection

With the increase in credit cards, ATM machines, and electronic financial services, we are rapidly moving toward a cashless society. In 1996, one metropolitan newspaper reported that "thirty years from now, chips will be implanted in our bodies encoded with credit card, passport, drivers license, and other information. Other experts say it won't take that long."[152]

We are moving in that direction much quicker than most people realize. Huge financial institutions are merging. Laws in the United States now allow banks to move into the securities and insurance business. Banks, brokerage firms, and insurance companies can now merge.[153]

New World Order economists want a cashless society. When the government has total knowledge of how people are using their finances, that knowledge also gives the government control over one's life. Ultimately, the goal of the economic leaders of the New World Order is to have control over all government computers.[154]

Eventually, total worldwide financial control will become a reality and the person pulling the strings will be the Antichrist (called the "beast" in the Book of Revelation). He causes ". . . as many as do not worship the image of the beast to be killed and he causes all, the small and the great, and the rich and the poor, and the free man and the slaves, to be given a mark on their right hand, or on their forehead, and he provides that no one should be able to buy or sell, except the one who has the mark, either the name of the beast or the number of his name" (Revelation 13:15-17 NASB).

How will the mark of the Antichrist be imprinted on a person's "right hand" or "forehead?" Technology is increasing at an exponential rate. One prediction made in 1996, of an implanted chip (which is encoded with all of our personal information), is already becoming outdated. We now have "nanotechnology [which] is the science of creating molecular-size machines that manipulate one atom at a time.... Nanotechnology comes from nanometer, or a billionth of a meter; a typical virus is about 100 nanometers across. ... The advent of programmable, nanoscale machines, will extend the Internet to things the size of molecules that can be injected under the skin, leading to Internet-enabled people." (*Time* Magazine, June 19, 2000, p. 96, 94, 102).

Even in the area of world trade, we can see advances toward interdependence or a one-world economy. Consider the following statement from a newspaper: "Beijing. After 13 years of fitful talks and six days of grueling bargaining, Chinese and U.S. negotiators signed a breakthrough agreement today that would remove trade barriers and clears the biggest hurdle to China's entry into the World Trade Organization."[155]

There was a time when Americans considered the U.S. stock market and economy financially separate from the rest of the world. This is no longer the case. An interdependent, global economy now exists.

In 1999, European countries developed and implemented a common currency known as the "Eurodollar." Europe is becoming financially unified. This is just one phase of a developmental progression toward a revived Roman Empire, which will consist of the ten most powerful nations of the European Union.

Europe originated or came out of the old Roman culture. "Europe's own choice for a national symbol is a woman riding on a beast."[156] In order to understand the significance of this image, turn to Revelation 17, "... and I saw a woman sitting on a scarlet beast, full of blasphemous names, having seven heads and ten horns. And the woman was clothed in purple and scarlet, and adorned with gold and precious stones and pearls, having in her hand a gold cup full of abominations and of the unclean things of her immorality" (Revelation 17:3-4 NASB). The image chosen to represent Europe, came from the Greek goddess Europa.[157] The symbol is a woman riding a bull. It originated in mythology and is identical to the symbol in Revelation 17. In the Bible, the woman represents a pagan world religion and the beast is the government of the Antichrist. The revived Roman Empire is represented by that government.

Global Unity

As we have seen, the movement toward a one-world government exists in several areas. It was shown through environmental and social programs such as Agenda 21 and the global commons. We can see the trend in paganism and nature worship. We then reviewed the financial world connection and trend toward a cashless society. The last point was the financial unification of Europe with its mythological national symbol. This parallels the symbol used by the Bible, which represents a false religion and the government of the Antichrist.

This movement towards globalization is progressing quickly. "The groundwork is being laid today for a worldwide computer banking system that will permit one man to control the entire population of the world."[158]

Throughout this chapter, we have covered the effects of the media on our culture and the movement toward a one world government. This development is covered from a human perspective.

The next chapter brings us to the development of a one world religious system. Chapter Four reviews the beast in the book of Revelation and Chapter Five summarizes the harlot that rides the beast.

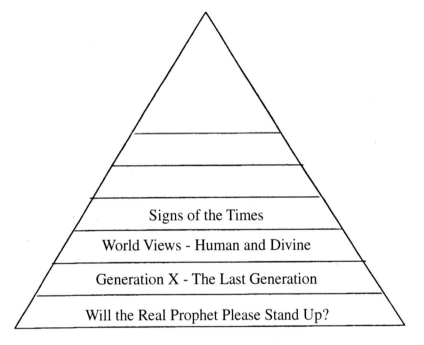

- FIVE -

NEW AGE APOSTASY: DEPARTURE FROM THE FAITH

"For the time will come when they will not endure sound doctrine; but wanting to have their ears tickled, they will accumulate for themselves teachers in accordance to their own desires."
II Timothy 4:3 NASB

This chapter explores the New Age movement and its spiritual implications. It examines the gospel and prophecy from the New Age viewpoint. Chapters 3 and 4 covered world views from man's perspective and the impact of an exponential increase in knowledge and technology. Just as in Chapter 4 the foundation for a world government is established, so in Chapter 5 the foundation for a world religion is established. This world religious system is referred to as the "great harlot" (Revelation 17:2-6).

NEW AGE: AN ANCIENT RELIGION IN DISGUISE

How popular is the New Age movement and what is encompassed by it? Take note of the religion section of a bookstore. You might find one shelf devoted to Bibles or Biblical literature, compared to eight or more shelves devoted to New Age books. This movement also permeates other areas such as psychology, philosophy, and self help.

The New Age movement is very broad. It covers many areas, including parapsychology, astrology, psychic phenomena, extrasensory perception (ESP), UFO's, and the occult, to name a few. Although the New Age movement includes many areas, some common beliefs include: a universal force, a god within all men, reincarnation, and a "belief that Jesus and the Christ consciousness are two separate entities and that the Christ is an office rather than a man."[159]

New Age philosophy is so accepted and widespread that it influences the vast majority of the population. People are influenced without even being aware of it. Highly educated people are following occult practices; thirty years ago, it would have only been a consideration by a population that had little or no education.

Two recent first ladies were involved in occultic practices. Hillary Clinton, an attorney, conducted seances and tried to contact the spirits of dead people. Mrs. Clinton "considers herself a 'committed Christian' and a 'serious reflective and prayerful woman,' but on weekends she likes to chat with Mahatma Gandhi and Eleanor Roosevelt. --- Nancy Reagan used astrologers, whom she believed could help guide the nation."[160]

Occultic practices are now accepted by the educated population. Our nation is not moving closer to the God of our forefathers, but is moving closer to the "god of this world."

As mentioned earlier, our belief system is built on one of two foundations or kingdoms. There is not a third foundation. On one end of the New Age spectrum we have witchcraft and paganism. This is obviously built on Satan's kingdom. The other end of the New Age spectrum is still demonic, but much more subtle.

The Eastern culture has always been open to various forms of the occult. Now the West is also mushrooming in occult practices. The generation that grew up in the sixties has been exposed to a distorted and anti-Biblical world view. This anti-Biblical world view has permeated Christian churches to such an extent that they have been targeted for conversion by pagans.[161] For example, a group called the Temple of Understanding, associated with the Gaia Institute and the United Nations Global Committee of Parliamentarians on Population Development, "is behind a new push to inundate Christian churches with nature worshiping propaganda."[162]

New Age Cloaks Occult

One end of the New Age spectrum is very subtle and easily disguises the occult. The occult, by definition, means secretive or hidden from view. It hides under the cloak of "New Age Enlightenment."

The West has picked up Eastern occult practices due to an increasing dissatisfaction with life. Science and established religions have not provided answers, especially for those growing up during and after the 1960's. "Instead of turning to Christ and His church, they are filling their spiritual world with old-fashioned occultism dressed in the modern garb of parapsychology, . . . Eastern mysticism, and numerous cults marching under the banner of the new age movement."[163]

The New Age movement has a strong appeal. Shirley MacLaine's beliefs are a good example of the New Age mentality. MacLaine's beliefs are based on her new realization about prior extraterrestrial visitations to earth. According to one reporter, "This realization came to her during a gradual process of becoming acquainted and accepting other non-mainstream ideas like reincarnation, spiritualism and channeling, eastern meditation, etc., which led to her experience of a divine cosmic energy, or God-force, which she says exists within all of us."[164]

This appeal to be "like God" is the same appeal Satan used in the Garden of Eden. "The new age pitch is the oldest lie of Satan; 'you will be like God' (Genesis 3:5)."[165] The great appeal of Satan's kingdom is to become like God or become God. The emphasis is always self-centered toward pride or pleasure. The appeal is one of self-deification. This is a prominent theme in New Age literature.

Do All Roads Lead to Rome?

The teaching that there are many paths to God and salvation is a lie straight from hell. A central belief of the New Age movement is that all religions are variations of expressions of the same God from different perspectives, from different prophets and at different times in history. No one religion is more accurate or correct than any other since each person defines his own truth.[166]

The New Age movement attempts to water-down Christianity. It dilutes it, reinterprets it, or denies it. Let's look at what the Bible says for understanding.

God commanded Adam and Eve not to eat the fruit of one tree in the Garden of Eden. They could eat of any other tree but one. If they were to eat of it, they would die. This is a physical death and a spiritual death that would result from sin (disobeying God). Satan, in the form of a serpent, approaches Eve and challenges God's Word (He is still challenging God's Word). "And the serpent said to the woman, 'you surely shall not die! For God knows that in the day you eat from it your eyes will be opened, and you will be like God knowing good and evil." (Genesis 3:4-6 NASB) Let's look at each point of this dialogue.

1. "**You surely shall not die**." Satan is saying "don't believe God. He lied to you."
2. "**The day you eat from it you will be like God**." He appealed to her pride, a desire to be like God. He lied to Eve and tempted her that she would be exalted and be equal to God.
3. "**[K]nowing good and evil**." This is true. She now had the knowledge of good and evil.

Note that Satan inserted one true statement with two false statements. Satan still operates in the same fashion. "... for he is a liar, and the father of lies" (John 8:44 NASB). "... Satan disguises himself as an angel of light" (II Corinthians 11:14 NASB). He lies and disguises himself. He gives enough truth so you will believe the lies that are mixed in with it.

Universalism is a lie. It promotes the belief that there are many paths to God. While this may be a "politically correct" theology in our day, it is the neopaganism of the New Age. People who buy into universalism are risking where they will spend eternity on a gamble that the Bible is wrong.[167] Jesus said, "... I am the way, and the truth and the life; no one comes to the Father, but through Me" (John 14:6 NASB).

This brings us to our source of authority. What is our standard or reference point to distinguish truth from error? "The Unitarian Universalist movement holds that personal experience, conscience, and reason should be the final authorities in religion. The Unitarian Universalist Church claims that, in the end, religious authority lies not in a book, or person, or institution, but in the self."[168]

In order to accurately assess the Universalist (and new age) position, we need to return to the basics. In Chapter 1, the reliability of the Bible was reviewed. Although there is a mountain of evidence to back up the authority of the Bible as God's Word, the one we emphasized was prophecy fulfillment. After establishing the Bible as our foundation, we saw the dangers of using "self" as a reference point in Chapter 4. The philosophers who taught that truth lies in one's experience led many people into despair and meaninglessness.

Thus, the Universalist position that "religious authority lies not in a book ... but in the self," is erroneous. It does not provide any reliable road to the truth. Truth gained through personal experience with self as the reference point may be quite different than someone else's truth. This truth is subjective rather than an objective reality.

Truth does exist as an objective reality, grounded in history and revealed in a book (the Bible). This reality consists of Biblical revelation and was historically revealed in the person of Jesus Christ. "For in Him all things were created, both in the heavens and on earth, visible and invisible, whether thrones or dominions or rulers or authorities – all things have been created through Him and for Him and He is before all things, and in Him all things hold together" (Colossians 1:16-17 NASB). This is a reality regardless of one's personal experience or human reasoning.

True Christianity is not a man-made religion, but involves a personal relationship with Jesus Christ. God loved you so much that He sent His Son to pay the price for your sins through His death on a cross. The only thing He requires is that you believe in Him (John 3:16) and then you ask Him into your life and accept His forgiveness of your sins (Revelation 3:20). You can do that right now by prayer using your own words. He knows your heart. Salvation is a gift and cannot be earned (Ephesians 2:8-9) but must be accepted (Revelation 3:20).

THE GOSPEL ACCORDING TO THE NEW AGE

When we look at the New Age movement and literature, it is important that we stay grounded in God's Word as our reference point. Any reference point that originates from self or personal experience will throw us off track.

Remember that Satan's mode of operation involves lying, distorting or reinterpreting. The New Age Gospel is an example of Satan interpreting and distorting God's Word.

According to Redfield, author of *The Celestine Prophecy*, "All the things you took for granted now need new definition, especially the nature of God and your relationship to God."[169] Redfield's book helps provide those new definitions, according to his view.

The opening page of *The Celestine Prophecy* quotes Daniel 12:3-4. "And those who have insight will shine brightly like the brightness of the expanse of Heaven, and those who lead the many to righteousness, like the stars forever and ever. But for you, Daniel, conceal these words and seal up the book until the end of time. Many will go back and forth, and knowledge will increase."

This book quotes God's Word yet has nothing to do with God's Word or the correct interpretation of the prophecy given to Daniel by God. From a Biblical perspective, this book is an example of distorting God's Word.

A number of sources within the New Age literature attempt to create their own gospel and then attempt to use the Bible to back their beliefs. Barbara Hubbard, author of *The Revelation*, "helps us" redefine what God really meant by some of the names and terms in the Bible. She states, "These words, 'Virgin Mary,' 'Jesus,' 'the elect,' 'Israel,' the 'New Jerusalem,' must be reinterpreted now. They do not relate to doctrines, ideologies, institutions, powers, or principalities. They relate to human potentials in every person on Earth."[170]

Again we come to the question of authority. What authority gives Hubbard the right to redefine these Biblical terms? Her answer is in the preface of her book, *The Revelation*. "This book, and the larger Book of Co-Creation from which it comes, was inspired by my direct experience of Christ in 1980.... I experienced the Christ as a living presence guiding us through the great transition to universal life. He seemed to me to be our potential self."[171]

Her authority is based on her personal experience with "the Christ" whom she defined as our "potential self." She relies on her own experience, in which she is the reference point.

What does God's Word say about her redefinition of His terms? "But know this first of all, that no prophecy of Scripture is a matter of one's own interpretation" (II Peter 1:20 NASB).

Scripture interprets scripture, not voices or visions. If a person's experience confirms God's Word, it is valid. If the experience contradicts or redefines God's Word, it is not from God. God does not contradict Himself. "... any kingdom divided against itself is laid waste" (Matthew 12:25 NASB).

What does the New Age gospel believe about man's basic nature? Hubbard's personal experience provides the answer, a quote allegedly from Jesus. She states that Jesus told her, "I, Jesus, have come to inform you that humanity is innocent of the conscious intent to reject God. You have been infected by a disease of a higher being other than your own. --- This awareness of your innocence is essential for your salvation."[172]

Once again we look to Scripture. Can Hubbard's quote, attributed to Jesus, be validated by God's Word? The answer is an emphatic "no." Genesis 8:21 says ". . . for the intent of man's heart is evil from his youth. . . ." Again, Romans 3:23 says, "For all have sinned and fall short of the glory of God."

Again the Bible contradicts the New Age gospel. This gospel (New Age) has a supernatural power and purpose that serves as its driving force. As shown, it is contrary to God's Word and is fueled by the demonic world, Satan's kingdom.

In the coming tribulation period, a horrible time of judgment (Matthew 24:21-22), a man will come to power who will rule the world. He will be the epitome of evil (empowered by Satan) and will deceive many people (II Thessalonians 2:4-10).

Some New Age authors prepare us for the Antichrist, but in a deceptive way. *The Celestine Prophecy* says the following about the future coming of a great man of God. "[S]ometime in history one individual would grasp the exact way of connecting with God's source of energy and direction and would thus become a lasting example that this connection is possible."[173] Could Redfield, unknowingly, be referring to the future Antichrist? Draw your own conclusion.

What makes the New Age gospel so attractive to many people when we already have the Gospel of Jesus Christ? One explanation is that the acceptance of the Biblical Gospel is also an acceptance of a responsibility to our Creator. Most of mankind refuses to acknowledge or accept that responsibility.[174]

The alternative gospel of the New Age requires no responsibility. This is more appealing and is in line with what the Bible predicts. "For the time will come when they will not endure sound doctrine; but wanting to have their ears tickled, they will accumulate for themselves teachers in accordance to their own desires" (II Timothy 4:3 NASB). Sadly, many people are looking for knowledge and power in all the wrong places.

Remember, there are two foundations and two kingdoms. One is God's kingdom and is built on a rock. The other is Satan's kingdom and is built on sand. If Satan deceives you into believing a lie, he controls that area of your life.[175]

Prophecy According to the New Age

Our focus has been on Biblical prophecy, the reliability of the Bible, and how to discern a counterfeit belief system from God's truth as revealed in His Word. We have established through God's Word that there are two supernatural kingdoms. One is God's Kingdom built on a rock foundation (Jesus Christ and God's Word). The other is Satan's kingdom built on a foundation of lies without substance. Satan, the father of lies, attacks God's truth in every area. Satan disguises himself as an angel of light (II Corinthians 11:14). This disguise is evident in the New Age movement.

Let's look at some New Age predictions of the future. Watch for some similarities with Biblical prophecies; watch also for the distortions and wrong predictions.

New Age Prediction:
• The government will make an official announcement of contact with extraterrestrials in 1997-1998.
Commentary:
While contact with ET's may happen in the future, it has not happened during the decade of the nineties.

New Age Prediction:
• There will be an increase in earthquakes, but not a huge rise in water levels, as Mother Earth cleanses herself.

Commentary:
The increase in earthquakes is Biblical (Luke 21:11). The "Mother Earth" concept is pagan.

New Age Prediction:
• A New World Order aims to be in power by 2003. There will be a banking system collapse and a central system established.
Commentary:
In the tribulation period, a New World Order will be established with a central economic system (Revelation 13:15-18).

New Age Prediction:
• Some people will "checkout" because of their inability to handle higher frequencies or energies.[176]
Commentary:
The "checkout" theory is a false prophecy to explain away the Rapture of the true Church (Commentary by author).

As stated earlier, Satan loves to weave some truth into a network of lies. In *Planet Earth: The Final Chapter*, Hal Lindsey quotes Hitler who said, "The best lie contains just enough truth to make it palatable." Hitler is a foreshadow of the Antichrist.

In New Age literature, Jesus is never called Messiah or Savior. Rather, He is referred to as a great man, one whom we all have the potential to be, a Christ. Jesus Christ is removed and a New Age Christ, or none at all, is substituted.[177]

Numerous New Age authors predict a "rapture" when large numbers of people disappear. Some New Age writers describe this disappearance as space ships removing people like the "Beam me up, Scotty" in the Star Trek series. Others talk in terms of "vibrations" accelerating until people disappear. In *The Revelation*, Hubbard states, "Those vehicles which you have called UFO's are moving in ultrahigh frequencies, and they slow down to 'appear' and quicken to 'disappear.' You shall do the same, and shall be taken up in the fullness of time in those vehicles in your quickened condition."[178]

Another example of the New Age rapture is in Redfield's book, *The Celestine Prophecy*, where people disappear through vibration levels. "Whole groups of people, once they reach a certain level, will suddenly become invisible to those who are still vibrating at a lower level. It will appear to the people on this lower level that the others just disappeared, but the group themselves will feel as though they are still right here only they will feel lighter."[179]

These quotes are from only two authors regarding a future disappearance of a large population. Many other New Age authors make the same predictions by way of space ships or vibration frequencies.

Going back to our reference point, the Bible, we can assess this New Age prediction. The Bible does refer to a "Rapture" which means "caught up." This is when Jesus Christ removes his true followers from this planet to be with Him. The Bible describes this event in the following way. "For the Lord Himself will descend from heaven with a shout, with the voice of the archangel, and with the trumpet of God; and the dead in Christ shall rise first. Then we who are alive and remain shall be caught up together with them in the clouds to meet the Lord in the air, and thus we shall always be with the Lord" (I Thessalonians 4:16-17 NASB). This great disappearance, referred to as the Rapture, will happen but it will not be the result of vibration levels or UFO's.

Satan is preparing an unbelieving world for this event, so people who are left behind, who live during the tribulation period, can somehow explain it away. Once again, he is distorting God's Word through the New Age prophets, so the people left behind after the Rapture will believe a lie.

Mystery Babylon, the Harlot

This section, Mystery Babylon, the Harlot, will cover the following points.

- Babylon the Great refers to a worldwide false religious system.
- This religious system will be occultic.
- It has its roots in ancient Babylon, which was characterized by the occult.
- The revival of the Roman Empire of Jesus' day parallels the revival of a Babylonian occultic worldwide religion.
- The New Age is inclusive of many occultic and pagan beliefs and will probably be a prominent part in the formulation of this religious system.
- This religious system will have a hatred for Jesus Christ and His true followers.
- The New Age not only includes occult and pagan beliefs but will have scientific overtones (the line between science and religion will be blurred).
- The creation of modern day Europe uses a pagan symbol as its national image which is identical to the Biblical image of "Babylon the Great."

There will be a political revival of the old Roman Empire of Jesus' day, by way of a ten nation empire (Daniel 2:42; Revelation 17:12). There will also be a spiritual unification into a one world religion.

Although the political Roman Empire fell, the spiritual Roman Empire continued to live. It became a spiritual "Roman Empire of popes" which ruled over the kings of Europe through the Dark Ages. This Roman Church martyred many thousands of Christians for refusing to accept that doctrine.[180]

The future spiritual Rome will be symbolized during the tribulation period as "Babylon the Great, the Mother of Harlots and of the Abominations of the Earth" (Revelation 17:5 NASB). This woman is a symbol of a worldwide false religious system.

The city of ancient Babylon was unified as a world religious system. The occult practices of ancient Babylon included: "black magic, demon contact, seances, miraculous materializations, astrology, and sorcery."[181]

Revelation 17:1-18 makes reference to seven kingdoms (or kings). "Five are fallen, one is, the other has not yet come; and when he comes, he must remain a little while" (Verse 10). In John's day, the five kingdoms that "are fallen" referred to: Assyria, Egypt, the neo-Babylonian empire of Daniel's day, Medo-Persia and the Greek empire. The "one that is" referred to the Roman Empire in John's day. The one that has "not yet come" refers to the future Antichrist and the revived Roman Empire.

The dominant religious theme that runs through the six previous empires is the occult. It will reach worldwide into a united religious system. This religious system will be eclectic. It will include the New Age, Eastern religions, mysticism, pantheism, and Christianity in a one world religious system which excludes God.[182] This tolerant, New Age, Eastern religious system hates a common enemy. That common enemy is Jesus Christ and His followers. In reference to the Harlot, Babylon the Great (world religious system), the Book of Revelation says, "And I saw the woman drunk with the blood of the saints, and with the blood of the witnesses of Jesus . . ." (Revelation 17:6 NASB).

As mentioned previously, the dominant religious theme that has run through the great world empires, beginning with ancient Babylon, was astrology and the occult in its many forms. It will reach its peak in the last world empire – the revived Roman Empire. What will be the catalyst to unify this false world religion?

Willis Harman, former consultant to the National Goals Research Staff of the White House, spoke of a potential bond that could unite the world. He believed that only one idea would prove strong enough to do this. "He pointed to the startling discoveries in the area of psychic powers, ESP, parapsychology, telekinesis, and telepathic communication and said that only the global acceptance of these new powers can bring humankind together."[183] These "new powers" have scientific overtones. They cannot really be proven or understood scientifically, but they look like science and their allure is personal empowerment. They fit nicely under the New Age umbrella.

This New Age umbrella attempts to unite religion and science. A news article interviewed Dr. Fielding, a Unitarian minister, and stated the following: "' I predict that [union of science and religion] because I see a hunger that I don't think the mainline or even the fundamentalist churches can deal with in an age of science.' Unitarian Universalists are comfortable with the concept of religion and science being linked, an attribute the Rev. Dr. Fielding believes will appeal to people of this information and technology age."[184] The article continues, "In one fellowship, pagan, Jewish, Christian and Eastern faiths, such as Hinduism and Buddhism, might be explored and accepted."[185] The line between science and religion becomes blurred; the line between world religions also becomes blurred.

World empires since ancient Babylon have a common belief system in the occult, which includes, but is not limited to, astrology, witchcraft, sorcery, demon contact, and paganism. Thirty years ago, paganism would have been considered an ancient religion linked to idolatry and the Old Testament. Paganism has become increasingly acceptable in our day and time. For example, earth worship is a pagan belief. For thousands of years, the earth has been considered a living being. Earth worship has involved numerous cultures. The ancient Greeks worshiped many gods and goddesses, including Gaia. She was a spirit with a physical body consisting of the earth itself. Gaia was the spirit of the planet earth.[186]

Near the end of the 20th century, the New Age philosophy of Pantheism re-emerged. There is a growing New Age trend to view the planet earth as a living physical-spiritual entity. "A number of new age authors echo this notion that 'Mother Earth' is undergoing a beneficial cleansing in order to purge herself of the 'pollution' that resides on her body."[187]

This return to pantheism can be seen as part of the reuniting of Babylon the Great. When examining signs of this reunification, a short review of the formation of today's Europe is necessary. In 1948, the Benelux Treaty began the European Customs Union. The 1957 Treaty of Rome created modern Europe.[188] As mentioned, the image representing Europe is the goddess Europa, from a Greek myth. Europe's national symbol is a woman riding on a beast. Revelation 17:3-5 says, ". . . And I saw a woman sitting on a scarlet beast . . . having in her hand a gold cup full of abominations and of the unclean things of her immorality, . . . and upon her forehead a name was written, . . . Babylon the Great, the Mother of Harlots and of the Abominations of the Earth." The same symbol represents Europe and the one world religion.

This one world religion will use mysticism and science to achieve credibility. New Age beliefs, without the power of the supernatural, would not last. The one world religion is empowered by Satan and his kingdom.

In the days of Moses and the ten plagues, we have examples of Satan's power. Many of the miraculous signs and plagues by God through Moses were imitated by the Egyptian magicians, empowered by Satan. Although the magicians performed similar miracles, they were weak by comparison, but nevertheless were empowered by Satan.

Signs and miracles will be performed by the Antichrist and the false prophet who are empowered by Satan (Revelation 13:4, 12-15). One characteristic of the last days is a rise in drug use and witchcraft. In Revelation 9:21, the word "sorceries" comes from a Greek word which means "pharmacy" and refers to both the occult and the use of drugs. The rate of drug use by teenagers has more than doubled since 1992.[189]

When examining "Babylon the Great," the one world religion, we return to our reference point, the Bible. It is easy to see that this worldwide religion and its different beliefs are false. Chapter 17 of Revelation describes this religion as worldwide (verses 1-2) and characterized by its hatred of Jesus and His followers (verse 6). Its destruction is described in Revelation, chapter 18.

Because occult miracles will mislead many, it is important to test the spirits. One of the hallmarks of the true God is that only He has the ability to predict the future with 100% accuracy. Satan's knowledge is confined to the past and the present. The worldwide false religion, Babylon the Great, will be destroyed (Revelation 18) because it is a creation of Satan's kingdom, built on the wrong foundation.

ONE WORLD GOVERNMENT - ONE WORLD RELIGION - ONE TRIGGER

The stage is set for a one world government and a one world religion. Both are symbolized by the image of the harlot, Babylon the Great, riding on a beast. The harlot represents the false world religion and the beast represents the revived Roman Empire and the Antichrist. He is identified with a one world government (Revelation 17:3, 11-12).

As shown, the stage for the one world government is set. The groundwork has been laid by the knowledge explosion, the high tech communication systems, the "Babel reversal" (communication across languages), and finally the manipulation of the media.

We have also seen how the stage is set for a one world false religion. We have explored the New Age movement, its scope, acceptance, and popularity. We have reviewed the movement away from the true God and His Word through universalism and the increase in the occult. We have seen how the New Age distorts God's Word to form a New Age gospel and their own predictions of the future to deceive large populations. The re-emergence of ancient paganism has become acceptable in many different forms. With the stage set to activate both a world government and a world religion, the next step requires a catalyst or a cataclysmic event. The current status could be compared to the completion of the electrical wiring in a large building. Nothing is left undone. In order to activate the power within the building, a switch has to be thrown.

That trigger mechanism could be a number of possible events. One possibility is a UFO threat. Lalonde emphasizes the importance of this event by making reference to a meeting in 1985 between Ronald Reagan and Mikhail Gorbachev. In a discussion between world leaders on ways to end the cold war, Reagan stated, **"If suddenly there was a threat to this world from some other species from another planet, we'd forget all the little local differences that we have between our countries, and we would find out once and for all that we are really all human beings on this earth together."**[190]

This, as we will see in our next section, is a very likely reality. Whitley Strieber, a well-known author and expert in the area of UFO phenomenon, believes that one undeniable UFO sighting would have a major global impact. ". . . [A] global, ecumenical religion that generates 'beliefs so broad in their scope and deep in their impact' could be built around a UFO motif. All that is needed, according to Strieber is 'a single undeniable sighting.'"[191]

The goals of the New Age movement involve creating world peace through a one-world spiritual system and a one-world governmental system with a leader of their choosing. Their covert goals are to destroy all systems based on the Bible in the beginning of the Age of Aquarius, 2000 A.D.[192]

COINCIDENCE OR DIVINE PROVIDENCE?

According to the Bible, certain events have to occur within the end times or the last generation. Some of these events include:
- A worldwide government formed through peaceful agreement.
- It must comprise the territory of the old Roman Empire. The Bible uses an image of a woman riding a beast as its symbol.

- The rebirth of Israel during the same generation as the revival of the old Roman Empire.

"The model for the modern state of Europe was born in 1948 - the same year as the rebirth of Israel. It was codified nine years later by what is known as the Treaty of Rome. --- Europe's own choice for a national symbol is a woman riding on a beast."[193]

If we are the generation spoken of by Jesus in the parable of the fig tree, then all of these events must occur during our generation. Either they have already happened or they are coming soon. The likelihood of the coincidental happening of these events simultaneously in the same generation is slim to none. This generation is the last generation before the Lord returns.

In conclusion, Chapter 5 has taken us through a modernized, updated version of paganism known as the New Age Movement. It is a return to the Tower of Babel on a high tech, worldwide scale.

The world is wired technologically and spiritually to become unified under one ruler. As we add one more level to our pyramid, we move into Chapter 6, which provides the trigger event. This event will move the world rapidly toward the tribulation period.

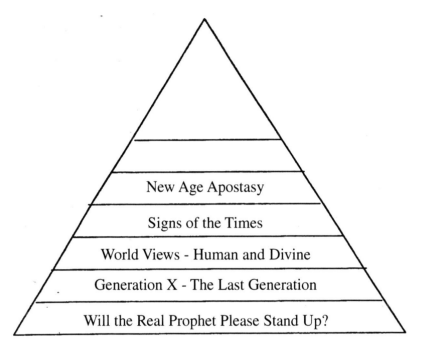

- SIX -

UFO'S! EXTRATERRESTRIALS! MILLIONS MISSING!

"... Because they did not receive the love of the truth so as to be saved. And for this reason God will send them a deluding influence so that they might believe what is false."
II Thessalonians 2:10-11 NASB

The preceding five chapters have set the world's stage for the remaining two chapters. These two chapters will cover future events of prophecy, climaxing with the glorious Second Coming of Christ. Chapter 6 will cover the "trigger event" referred to in the preceding chapter. We will cover this event from both the Biblical description and the New Age description. The New Age description of this event will become one of the greatest worldwide deceptions mankind has ever experienced.

DO UFO'S REALLY EXIST?

In the 1940's, no one believed UFO's were from outer space. According to a 1947 Gallup poll, "Most thought they were illusions, hoaxes, secret weapons, or phenomena that could be explained."[194] Contrast this with a more "recent Gallup poll which revealed that 72 percent of Americans believe in extraterrestrial life; 48 percent believe in UFO's and 15 percent believe they have seen a UFO. According to other polls, up to 3 percent believe they have been abducted by a UFO."[195]

The March 2000 cover of *Life* magazine was on the subject "UFOs – Why do we believe?" In this issue of *Life*, on page 48, "The Search for Extraterrestrial Life," contained the following statement:

> Meanwhile, according to a *Life* poll, 30 percent of us think aliens have already landed. The number of Americans who say they have been abducted is "staggering," says one St. Louis psychiatrist. Harvard Medical School's John Mack has treated hundreds and has a new book out. There are 300 UFO organizations, 38 UFO magazines. China reportedly has 40,000 ufologists.

The UFO – Extraterrestrial phenomenon is a current reality, accepted by many. The belief system in UFO's has increased considerably in popularity over the last 50 years. This growing acceptance of the UFO phenomenon and extraterrestrial life is based on mountains of evidence, reported sightings and accounts of abductions. Excluding newspapers, the number of professional articles exceeds 6,000 in English, 2,200 in foreign journals, and 1,350 periodicals on UFO's.[196]

Despite many unconfirmed testimonies, frauds, and disinformation, there is too much solid credible evidence to ignore. Let's look at a few examples out of the thousands reported.

The Mexico Flap

Mexico City became the site of one of the best documented reports of UFO sightings in recorded history. The event occurred on January 1, 1993 at 2:00 p.m. On this date, thousands of people sighted a UFO during the daytime. Reports swamped radio stations; televison stations broadcast the sighting. Traffic was snarled as people left their cars to view the shiny metal disc in the sky.[197]

Even though it was publicized, documented, and eye witnessed, it was not reported in the U.S. news. There were also numerous videotapes of the incident.

Since the early 1990's, many UFO sightings have occurred over Mexico. The sightings have been by pilots, citizens and government authorities. "Although the sightings have been thoroughly covered in the Mexican press, . . . the majority of the populace has become desensitized to their presence and . . . view the sightings as 'routine.' While opinions vary, many of the witnesses believe that the Mexican flap represents the fulfillment of ancient Mayan or biblical prophesies."[198] A "flap" is a large number of sightings in a short period of time.

The Israel Flap

Since 1996, there have been hundreds of reports in Israel of sightings of UFO's. According to *UFO Reality*, UFO's began to appear in 1996 in Israel, Iran, and Australia. Mass eye witness reports came in, including intervention by police and the army. "The succession of reports is so staggering that it is already impossible to keep track of the hundreds of thousands of eyewitness reports that pour in each day."[199]

One well-documented sighting occurred in 1996 in Israel. A group of 50 people watched a UFO at 2:30 a.m. One official described the event, ". . . like a giant tent full of lights, light up the sky above two residential districts. The UFO passed just over our heads at a height of not more than 100 – 200 meters. The event lasted close to ten minutes. Suddenly, without any advance warning, it disappeared."[200]

Israel is well known for its UFO sightings. "Israel is recognized as an international UFO hot spot – with an unsurpassed quantity and quality of evidence."[201]

Apollo 11 Sightings

Astronauts Neil Armstrong and Edwin Aldrin reported UFO sightings after their lunar landing. Their reports on July 21, 1969 were dismissed and went unconfirmed for years, as shown by the following excerpt.

> According to Otto Binder, a former NASA employee, the agency has a long standing policy of blocking sensitive transmissions through secret, non-public frequencies. According to Binder[202] an unnamed ham radio operator picked up the following transmission on a public bypass channel when Apollo 11 landed in the Sea of Tranquility:
>
> MISSION CONTROL: "What's there? . . . Mission control calling APOLLO 11."
>
> APOLLO 11: These babies are huge, Sir . . . enormous. . . . Oh, God, you wouldn't believe it! I'm telling you there are other spacecraft out there . . . . lined up on the far side of the crater edge . . . they're on the moon watching us. . . ."

In 1979, Otto Binder's account was confirmed by the former chief of NASA communications, Maurice Chatelain.[203]

In spite of Chatelain's senior position at NASA, it still denied his claims. In his book, *Our Cosmic Ancestors*, Chatelain makes a number of startling claims about UFO sightings during NASA missions.[204]

Roswell Incident

This is one of the best-known UFO events in history and is also one of the biggest cover-ups in history. The following will briefly review the incident at Roswell, New Mexico.

In July 1947, Mac Brazel, a local New Mexico rancher went to check his sheep after an intense thunderstorm the previous night. He discovered a lot of debris including a crashed disk and a shallow gouge several hundred feet long. He took the debris to authorities at Roswell Army Air Field.

On July 8, 1947, Colonel William Blanchard, Commander of the 509th Bomb Group issued an official press release about the "crashed disk." It appeared in many major U.S. newspapers.

Hours later a second press release was issued by General George Ramey, Commander of the Eighth Air Force at Fort Worth Army Air Field in Texas. This rescinded the first press release, claimed that Colonel Blanchard made a mistake, and described the debris and crashed disk as a "weather balloon and its radar reflector." This was followed by 50 years of cover up.

There was too much evidence to continue the cover up. In 1994, Steven Schiff, United States Congressman from New Mexico, told the press that he was stonewalled by the Defense Department regarding the 1947 Roswell event. Congressman Schiff, while planning to do a further investigation, said the Defense Department's refusal to respond was astounding and was another government cover-up.[205]

Since the Freedom of Information Act, further attempts were made to obtain UFO documents. The government claims they can't be released or don't exist. Government agencies have continued to hide behind national security. ". . . UFO's appear to involve the highest categories of security classifications available."[206]

Jimmy Carter, then Governor of Georgia, reported a UFO sighting in 1969. Then in 1976, as a presidential candidate, he pledged: "If I become president, I'll make every piece of information this country has about UFO's available to the public and the scientist." After he became president, he never said another word about it. He didn't deny it or confirm it. He ignored it.[207]

THE UFO WORLD VIEW

What we believe determines our behavior and attitudes. We have discussed historical world views from philosophy, psychology, and religion (which includes new age and occult beliefs). This brings us to a belief in UFO's and extraterrestrials.

We have only looked at the tip of the iceberg concerning UFO evidence and documentation. On top of the thousands of cases of UFO's reported over the last 50 years, "more than 700 of the cases have been reported by experienced airline and military pilots."[208] Most of the evidence in these cases is related to the credibility of the witness. Airline and military pilots are very credible witnesses when it comes to UFO sightings.

In the same way world views have changed over the last 50-100 years in areas such as philosophy and the New Age movement, people increasingly accept the reality of UFO's. For example, Missler and Eastman in their book, *Alien Encounters*, state, ". . . we have been conditioned by an unparalleled media fixation with UFO's and extraterrestrials. Now more than 75 percent of Americans believe extraterrestrials exist and have been visiting us for millennia."

The overwhelming evidence of UFO's and actual alien encounters, makes it difficult, if not impossible, to explain away. Furthermore, the government and military have taken extreme measures to cover it up.

Why are they covering up the evidence? On the one hand, the government attempts to cover up or explain it away. Yet, they claim it is in the interest of national security. In the interest of national security implies a fear of how people would react if they knew the truth.

The general belief in UFO's and extraterrestrials (ET's) is becoming so prevalent that people are conditioned toward acceptance of the whole UFO and ET phenomena. What does this belief mean and how does it affect me personally?

Missler and Eastman provide an answer. If UFO's and ET's are real, this "will lead to the biggest challenge ever faced by mankind. If these things are not real, they bear evidence of a gigantic delusion – one that is being orchestrated with a political end in sight. . . . what lies behind these strange events will soon affect every living person on this planet."[209]

ET'S AND THE NEW AGE PROPHETS

What is the origin of the universe and mankind? One scientific possibility is the Big Bang Theory that the universe came into being through "chance." The word chance, according to Random House Webster's College Dictionary, is "the unpredictable and uncontrolled element of an event or occurrence." Somehow through chance and then evolution, we have the universe and mankind.

A second explanation for the origin of the universe and mankind is creation. The Biblical account in the Book of Genesis tells us that "In the beginning God created the heavens and the earth" (Genesis 1:1 NASB). It also tells us that ". . . God created man in His own image . . ." (Genesis 1:27 NASB).

Some scientists have a problem dealing with the origin of life. On the one hand, they reject the creationist view. After all, it can't be understood scientifically. They also have a problem with the chance-probability explanation.

We now have a third explanation of the origin of life. Sir Fredrick Hoyle, a prominent astronomer, researched the spontaneous generation theory. In 1981, Hoyle expressed the following view:

> The likelihood of the formation of life from inanimate matter is one to a number with 40 thousand naughts (zeros) after it. It is enough to bury Darwin and the whole theory of evolution. . . . [I]f the beginnings of life were not random they must therefore have been the product of purposeful intelligence.[210]

Hoyle was among a small number of prominent scientists who believed that life was delivered from outer space either by aliens or comet, infected with bacteria. He did not accept the chance probability theory nor a miraculous cause for the origin of life.[211] Francis Crick, a brilliant molecular biologist, agreed with Hoyle.

Combine the beliefs of some scientists, who reject the chance – probability theories and the supernatural, with the belief in UFO's. The result is the Church of ET.

Missler and Eastman describe the Church of ET as the result of the UFO movement of the 1960's and 1970's. The theme of these UFO Churches is identical to those of Eric Von Daniken (author of *Chariots of the Gods*) and Sitchin. Life on earth was delivered and created by ET's. Humans are their children and the ET's are returning to help us evolve into the next stage of our evolutionary process.[212]

UFO and ET's, "the World's Reality"

It is next to impossible to deny that UFO's and ET's exist when one reviews the evidence. There are over 12,000 reports of UFO's that were reviewed by Project Bluebook since 1947. Although a majority of the reports were identified as natural or man-made, there are a significant number of reports that have no apparent earthly explanation.[213]

The belief in UFO's and ET's is growing; they are becoming accepted as an established fact. The current belief in UFO's was not even a consideration 50 years ago. Not only is there a growing acceptance by the mass population but there is also an acceptance by governmental agencies. According to Lalonde's book, *2000 A.D.*, the Federal Emergency Management Agency (FEMA) has a training manual that includes UFO situations. Chapter 13 of *The Fire Officers Guide to Disaster Control*, refers to the "very real threat posed by Unidentified Flying Objects (UFO's) whether they exist or not."

The existence of UFO's can hardly be questioned in this day and time. According to a Temple University history professor, the existence of UFO's is so well established that it isn't a matter to prove as was the case in the 1950's and 1960's.[214]

There are numerous reports of alien abductions or encounters. People have been abducted by aliens, physically examined, and have undergone surgical procedures. They have experienced amnesia, but under hypnosis they have total recall of the procedures. Many abductees have very similar experiences as recalled under hypnotic regression.

The kinds of reports that are fairly well documented are sometimes terrifying experiences for the abductees. The UFO phenomena and alien encounters of today were the material used for science fiction 40 to 50 years ago. "UFO's are real, . . . thousands of people around the world are receiving messages from them, and . . . these messages are forming the backbone of a new, powerful New Age religion of universalism and fellowship with entities many identify as aliens."[215]

Whether UFO's and ET's are real or not is only part of a mounting problem. What mankind believes is extremely powerful. ". . . [I]n today's world it is not so important whether UFO's exist as whether we believe they exist. And one in three Americans actually expects that we will be contacted by aliens within the next century."[216]

There are astronomers who are also open to the possibility of alien contact and how the world should prepare for such an event. Ian Crawford is an astronomer in the department of physics and astronomy at University College, London. "He believes that the cosmic perspective provided by the exploration of the universe argues for the political unification of our world. He explains, '... and if we do ever meet other intelligent species out there among the stars, would it not be best for humanity to speak with a united voice?'" (*Scientific American*, July 2000, "Where Are They?" Ian Crawford).

Ancient Visitors or Astronauts?

Although the UFO phenomena and the belief in ET's have grown rapidly over the last 50 years, there is evidence that they visited our planet thousands of years ago. Some of our most ancient records come from the Sumerians in the third millennium B.C.

> The history of Sumer has primarily been reconstructed from thousands of clay tablets. . . . Recorded . . . are stories of the "gods" which came down to earth from the heavens. Popular authors . . . have interpreted these texts as visitations by highly advanced "ancient astronauts" who flew to earth in spaceships and were worshiped as "gods" by virtually every ancient culture.[217]

We not only have written records of ancient visitors referred to as "gods," we also have archaeological accomplishments that are beyond our ability to duplicate in this day and time. One example is the Great Pyramid of Giza. Numerous teams of engineers, scientists, and architects have attempted to determine the methods used in its construction. Even with our current technology, these scientists have not been able to duplicate the architectural achievements of ancient Egypt.[218]

There are no records indicating why or how the Sphinx and pyramids were constructed. Recent archeological evidence indicates that the Sphinx and Great Pyramid may have been built over 12,000 years ago.[219]

We also have evidence of ancient rock paintings of alien-like creatures. In Australia, rock paintings depict "the mythical mouthless gods of creation, Vonjinda, the object of worship by ancient natives. . . . With their large oval heads and over-sized eyes, the resemblance to modern extra-terrestrials called 'Grays,' the aliens depicted in Steven Spielberg's blockbuster movie, *Close Encounters of the Third Kind*, is striking."[220]

How are we to interpret or understand ET's from past paintings that have striking similarities to current day descriptions reported by abductees? What kind of beings lived on this planet thousands of years ago that were more advanced technologically than our current scientists? What kind of being had the technology and power to construct the Great Pyramid, with stone blocks weighing almost 100 tons, and with specifications that "exceed the tolerances allowed for the tiles of the Space Shuttle?"[221]

Where is this line of questioning leading us? Could these ancient visitors be supernatural beings? What about human beings with extraordinary intelligence and strength? Some of the evidence points to both human and supernatural. Prepare for a mind-expanding journey.

Men and "Gods"

Is it really possible to have supernatural beings breed with humans? In order to answer this question, we once again turn to our true external point of reference, the Bible.

Genesis 6:2 says, ". . . the sons of God saw that the daughters of men were beautiful; and they took wives for themselves, whomever they chose." These "sons of God" are supernatural beings; they are not beings following God's will as shown in Genesis 6:5. "Then the Lord saw that the wickedness of man was great on the earth, and that every intent of the thoughts of his heart was only evil continually" (Genesis 6:5 NASB).

Greek and Roman mythology also speaks of this intermarrying. The Titans were the giant offspring of the gods and their human wives. "According to mythology they also assisted in the building of the magnificent monuments of Greece. . . . According to numerous authors, these 'mighty men' of the golden age were the 'third party' who assisted mankind in the building of the monuments of Egypt, Stonehenge, the Americas, and the Far East."[222]

Current studies in mythology usually show a nugget of truth at the core. We can find this, for example, in the mythological accounts of the flood found in the book of Genesis.

A copy of the Genesis Apocryphon, dating back to the second century B.C., was discovered at Qumran in 1947. "When scholars finally made public its content, the document confirmed that celestial beings from the skies had landed on planet Earth. More than that, it told how these beings had mated with earth women and had begat giants."[223]

Taking it one step further, let's examine Jacques Vallee's book, *Passport to Magonia*. Vallee examines the ancient records and folklore throughout history; in nearly every culture, there were recorded stories of beings who flew in the sky, abducted and interbred with humans. We, as humans, have a tendency to dismiss folklore, yet the stories of ancient times closely parallel the alleged encounters that have accelerated in the last part of the 20th century.[224]

In ancient times, the ET's were referred to as gods. In our day they are referred to as Aliens or ET's. What appears to be a common denominator both in ancient times, and in the Biblical account in Genesis 6, is an interbreeding of some form of ET and human beings.

There seems to be a relationship between the interbreeding accounts and the reports given by abductees, who have undergone physical exams by aliens. The abductees report entering the craft and being in a white room like an operating room. Then, they typically "report contact with the same gray skinned aliens who methodically perform head to toe examinations with special attention to the genital area. In hundreds of cases, women report being probed with long metallic devices in the abdominal or genital area."[225]

WHERE DO UFO'S AND ALIENS COME FROM?

While there is much evidence for the existence of UFO's and ET's, their origin is very controversial even among experienced UFO investigators. The common view is the "extraterrestrial hypothesis (ETH)." This is the belief that extraterrestrials come from another star system. However, in recent years, a number of prominent UFO researchers have challenged this hypothesis as a result of well-documented accounts of UFO's defying the laws of physics.[226]

Evidence points to UFO's being actual physical objects. There are also accounts of UFO's changing shape and dematerializing.

> UFO's have been tracked on radar traveling at over 25,000 miles per hour within our atmosphere. Yet, unlike physical objects, they do not cause sonic booms and they do not burn up. They have been known to make right angle turns at over 15,000 miles per hour, something no physical object could endure. And despite visual confirmation, UFO's often fail to show up on photographic film or radar devices.[227]

If UFO's are not permanent constructions of matter and if they do not travel by conventional means from one solar system to another, what are they? If the extraterrestrial hypothesis is rejected, what then?

Jacques Vallee offers an alternative explanation.

> If they are not spacecraft, what else could UFO's be? ... I believe that the UFO phenomenon represents evidence for other dimensions beyond space-time; the UFO's may not come from ordinary space but from a multiverse which is all around us.... I believe there is a system around us that transcends time and it transcends space. Other researchers have reached the same conclusion.[228]

Even if we consider the possibility that UFO's are constructed from some other form of hardware, where do they hide when not visible to human eyes? In 1950, nuclear physicist Enrico Fermi raised some interesting questions. "If extraterrestrials are commonplace, he asked, where are they? Should their presence not be obvious? This question has become known as the Fermi Paradox." (*Scientific American*, July 2000, "Where Are They?" Ian Crawford). These are questions asked from the standpoint of a three dimensional universe.

There have been UFO reports of encounters where the UFO materialized and dematerialized within our three dimensional space. Some observers have suggested UFO's might exist in a parallel universe, one orthogonal (at right angles) to our own.[229] Cosmologists Andrei Linde and Alex Vilenkin have "shown how certain mathematical assumptions lead, at least in theory, to the creation of a multiverse" (*Scientific American*, December 1999, "Exploring Our Universe and Others," Martin Rees).

The next question to explore in this discussion of UFO's, universe, multiverse, and aliens is: where does science end and religion or the supernatural begin? John Mack, a psychiatrist with more than 40 years of training, believes that the dualistic view of religion and science is breaking down. Mack views the phenomenon of UFO abduction "as a merging of science and religion, the appearance of a new paradigm of thought – one in which the lines separating faith and science, religion, philosophy, the material world, and the spirit world are blurred. The result . . . is a merging and unification of science, religion, philosophy, and the spiritual realm."[230] This loss of dualism in science and religion leads to a loss of dualism spiritually which moves us toward the New Age religion.

SCIENCE IN THE NEW AGE - HOW MANY DIMENSIONS?

Science has taken on a whole new meaning in modern times, especially in the area of physics. Out of the quantum theory and the theory of relativity, the new physics has emerged.[231]

Einstein's theory of relativity demonstrates that time, space, and motion interact. In other words, time is not a constant. It is considered a fourth dimension of reality.

We live in a three dimensional world. For illustration purposes, a two dimensional world is a drawing on a flat piece of paper. When you add a third dimension, we have depth. It is the difference between a square and a cube. Our three dimensional world includes length, width, and height. Our fourth dimension, time, is temporal.

Once we go beyond our three dimensional existence, we move into hyperspace. These dimensions are beyond our reality and may be more in line with a multiverse or parallel universe.

William Alnor, in *UFO's in the New Age*, describes the concept of a multiverse. Alnor refers to Albrecht and Alexander's work in the Spiritual Counterfeits Projects 1977 *Journal on UFO's*. They describe how UFO's could be the work of beings from another dimension. They describe and draw a two dimensional world, "Flatland." The two dimensional world would have a distorted view of objects from a three dimensional world (height, depth, width). Albrecht and Alexander take this a step further by asking the question, how would we, living in a three dimensional world, view objects from the fourth dimension?[232]

In other words, a being in hyperspace or in a dimension beyond our three dimensional existence would have capabilities and rules of their own geometry beyond our understanding. "Imagine a universe of only two dimensions: a flat plane. This imaginary universe is inhabited only by two dimensional beings – we'll call them Mr. and Mrs. Flat. They can only conceive of two dimensions since that is all they are capable of experiencing directly."[233] Any intrusion by us on their two dimensional existence would give them a distorted view of a three dimensional being. In other words, if you stick a pencil through a piece of paper with a picture of Mr. and Mrs. Flat on it, all they would see is a circle where the pencil goes through the paper (two dimensional or flat view).

We have only dealt with a two and three dimensional existence and touched on the fourth dimension. We now know from particle physics that we live in a universe of at least ten dimensions.[234]

Given the fact that UFO's tend to defy physics and the "nuts" and "bolts" descriptions, we can begin to look at dimensionality as another way to understand the UFO phenomenon. "With such a framework, UFO's can be viewed as an inter-dimensional phenomenon that can materialize and interact with us within our space-time domain."[235]

New Physics: Quantum What?

The quantum theory is extremely difficult and technical; an explanation will not be attempted here. This section looks at some of the possible implications and interpretations of the "New Physics" and how it applies to a New Age philosophy.

According to physicist Paul Davies, "uncertainty is the fundamental ingredient of the quantum theory. It leads directly to the consequences of unpredictability. . . . The quantum factor apparently breaks the chain by allowing effects to occur that have no cause."[236]

This breaking of cause – effect relationships is a conclusion reached when the rules of physics, as currently understood, do not answer man's questions in a way that makes sense to him. By definition, the word "effect" has the following meaning: "Something that is produced by an agency or cause; result; consequence" (*Random House Webster's College Dictionary*).

Let's consider one of the ramifications of breaking cause - effect relationships. If one cannot scientifically draw a conclusion in any particular area based on a cause - effect relationship, one must reason that something either does not exist, exists without a cause, or exists for no apparent reason. We can only know it (whatever "it" may be) by our experience. As we have already seen, we cannot rely on experience alone to confirm a reality. In the preceding section on dimensions, we saw how a being in hyperspace (beyond our three dimensional existence) could easily deceive us through our five senses. An example of this is the materializing and dematerializing of UFO's.

When experience alone becomes man's criteria for determining reality, he is a candidate for demonic deception. Disregarding cause – effect relationships helps lay the groundwork for such a deception to take place.

Some people have drawn erroneous conclusions about quantum theory, because of its complexity and their inability to completely understand it. For example, they erroneously believe that full account must be taken of quantum theory in the search to understand God and existence. An example of this can be seen in the following statement: "Many modern writers are finding close parallels between the concepts used in the quantum theory and those of Oriental mysticism, such as Zen. But whatever one's religious persuasions, the quantum factor cannot be ignored."[237]

The content of this statement suggests that man through science can potentially gain the knowledge necessary to understand God and existence. This also opens the door to mysticism or experience. It is interesting to note that when science (which is based on logic and cause-effect relationships) runs into an unknown, they become "religious." We are beginning to see the line between science and religion become very blurred.

Quantum theory forms one of the pillars of the "new physics and provides the most convincing scientific evidence yet that consciousness plays an essential role in the nature of physical reality."[238] By connecting consciousness to physical reality, we have a paradigm shift. Consciousness, or the perception of the observer, becomes more relevant than the external world. As stated by Paul Davies, in his book, *God and the New Physics*, "This mosaic of self-reference is the essential feature of consciousness."

What we now have is an emphasis on the importance of consciousness as opposed to an external reality. This leads directly into the evolution of consciousness which is a dominant theme in the New Age movement. What is also of interest is Davies' emphasis on "self-reference" as the "essential feature of consciousness." Chapter 3 reviewed the dangers of using "self" as a reference point instead of using God's Word as our standard.

When a scientist uses self as a reference point and applies science to understand infinite truths, he will inevitably run aground. He is attempting to reason his way into the infinite, an impossible task. Let's look at the attempt of one scientist to reason his way to the infinite.

> A God who is in time is, therefore, in some sense caught up in the operation of the physical universe. Indeed, it is quite likely that time will cease to exist at some stage in the future.... In that case God's own position is obviously insecure.... There is thus a grave and fundamental difficulty in reconciling all the traditional attributes of God. Modern physics --- drives a wedge between God's omnipotence and the existence of his personality.[239]

This is an example of man trying through reason to understand God. The following quote from the Bible is God's answer to the preceding statement. "'For My thoughts are not your thoughts, neither are your ways My ways,' declares the Lord. 'For as the heavens are higher than the earth, so are My ways higher than your ways, and My thoughts than your thoughts'" (Isaiah 55:8-9 NASB). Notice the emphasis in these two verses. It compares God's thoughts which are infinite, to man's thoughts which are finite. One is higher than the other. This barrier between finite and infinite thinking, cannot be crossed while in a temporal body. Attempting to cross that line is an attempt to become like God or to bring Him down to our level.

Ultimately, using self as a reference point, can lead to the New Age concept of One Universal Mind. An example of this is found in the following statement.

We could describe this state of affairs by saying that nature is a product of its own technology, and the universe is a mind: a self-observing as well as self-organizing system. Our own minds could then be viewed as localized "islands" of consciousness in a sea of mind, an idea that is reminiscent of the oriental conception of mysticism. . . .[240]

This section is not an argument against physics or quantum theory. It is to show what happens when a scientist reaches conclusions using himself as a reference point. He also has "an exaggerated trust in the efficacy of the methods of natural science applied to all areas of investigation." This is the definition of "scientism" as quoted from Miriam Webster's Collegiate Dictionary, 10th edition. In other words, "scientism" is putting too much trust in the methods of science and applying them to all other areas of investigation.

In contrast to Paul Davies' conclusions from his understanding of physics, let's look briefly at another view. Hugh Ross, who has a Ph.D. in astronomy and is also a minister, discusses science's limitations and his conclusions in his book, *Beyond the Cosmos*. He states, "In 1931 Australian mathematician Kurt Godel established that mathematical 'truths' exist for which we can develop no absolutely rigorous proofs. No set of axioms can be proven totally consistent. No set of axioms, then, is provably complete."[241] Ross goes on to say "perfect insight into the physics of the cosmos will always remain beyond our capability."[242] Note that he recognizes the limitations of science and man, yet he is a brilliant scientist. His book, *Beyond the Cosmos*, covers recent discoveries in astrophysics and what it reveals about God.

His reference point is God and His Word. He states: "The limits on our abilities to know truth and visualize truth merely remind us that we are the creatures, not the Creator. But the limits do not stop us from seeking to gain a clearer picture of who He is through studying both His inspired Word and His creative work."[243]

Aliens! Who Are They? What Are They Saying?

Considering the fact that aliens and UFO's appear to exist but do not fit into the extraterrestrial hypothesis (from another star system), what options are left? We have described the inter-dimensional possibility. This means that they have the capacity to move out of a higher dimension into our three dimensional world at will. Previously we described this in terms of "flatland," a two dimensional existence touched by a three dimensional object.

We have also discussed the duality of the universe. There are two kingdoms and two foundations. There is God's kingdom and Satan's kingdom. We can therefore conclude that these ET's or aliens fit into one of these two kingdoms.

The Bible never discusses UFO's or aliens, but does discuss fallen angels and demons. It would be reasonable to conclude that the manifestation of UFO's and aliens fits into Satan's kingdom and is the result of a demonic materialization to deceive mankind. The New Age literature reviewed so far concerning aliens and abductees has left out the message and gospel of Jesus Christ.

The "messages" that the contactees (humans on earth) receive from the "space brothers" (ET's) are distortions of God's Word concerning prophecy, if it is mentioned at all. According to Alnor, "the real giveaway to me that the extraterrestrial beings are giving contactees messages that could lead the world into delusion is that in each of their biblical parallels concerning the end times, they have carefully excised Jesus Christ from the picture and have substituted a new age Christ, or none at all."[244]

In every way the messages and the UFO religious movement reject traditional Judeo-Christian ideas about God, morality, and even reality itself, in favor of a new world order and an occult-based spirituality.[245] This UFO religious movement is included under the New Age umbrella.

A popular New Age – UFO writer, Brad Steiger has collected messages from the "space brothers" for years and included them in a book called, *The Fellowship*, a new type of bible. He wants the ideas to replace traditional Christianity with a new world occultic faith.[246]

The new world occultic faith is really old-fashioned paganism presented with a New Age disguise. As mentioned in the prior section, the UFO – occult movement tends to talk in pagan terms, especially when it concerns prophecy. Contactees receive messages regarding the need for Mother Earth to be cleansed. "According to hundreds of contactees, earth changes are part of a cleansing that could be catastrophic if our space brothers didn't intervene, but they will. The ET's we are told have a plan to salvage our planet and prevent Earth Mother from destroying the majority of life as she cleanses herself."[247]

UFO abductees are rarely, if ever, practicing Christians. Los Angeles Christian journalist Stuart Goldman made the following statement based on a lengthy investigation of Whitley Scriber, author of best sellers *Communion* and *Transformation*. In an unpublished manuscript, Goldman examined the background of UFO abductees. Almost all "have some background in new age or occultic beliefs. Interestingly, studies show that there are very few practicing Christians or Jews amongst UFO contactees. What could this mean? Are the aliens racist? Or does this, rather, indicate something about the belief systems of the abductees themselves?"[248]

The deception involved in the New Age movement is extremely powerful and is very subtle. It is seductive and deceptive enough to draw in born-again believers in Jesus Christ especially if they have moved away from God's Word (the true standard or reference point). Christians increasingly tend to combine their faith with New Age beliefs.[249]

The following surveys are reviewed in Jubilee magazine, Spring 2000. According to a 1999 Gallup poll, 39% of Americans describe themselves as born-again, evangelical Christians; 25% say they are fundamentalist while 15% say they are evangelical. Of those self-described born-again, evangelical Christians:

20% believe in reincarnation;
26% believe in astrology;
16% have visited a fortune teller; and
33% are pro-choice.

A survey of born-again Christians by the Barna Research Group (www.Barna.org), found that:

45% believe that if people are good enough, they can earn a place in heaven;
34% believe that Jesus committed sins like other people;
35% do not believe that Jesus was physically resurrected from the dead; and
45% believe that Satan is not a living being, but is a symbol of evil.

Clearly, some New Age beliefs affect most people to some degree.

Christians are referred to collectively as the "Bride of Christ" (II Corinthians 11:2). For a believer to play around with a false religion or belief system (i.e., new age, occult, witchcraft, etc.) is viewed throughout the Bible as spiritual adultery.[250]

THE UFO/RAPTURE CONNECTION

The stage is now set for the next major event in prophecy. Christians commonly refer to this event as the "Rapture." The word "Rapture" does not appear in the Bible. "The word 'rapture' comes from the Latin word rapios, which means literally, to be 'caught up' or 'snatched away.'"[251] The phrase "caught up" is found in I Thessalonians 4:17.

The Rapture happens instantly and is a sign-less event, in that it is not preceded by any particular sign. It is an event that happens in two stages. One Bible reference concerning the Rapture is as follows:

"For the Lord Himself will descend from heaven with a shout, with the voice of the archangel, and with the trumpet of God; and the dead in Christ shall rise first. Then we who are alive and remain shall be caught up together with them in the clouds to meet the Lord in the air, and thus we shall always be with the Lord" (I Thessalonians 4:16-17 NASB).

The "dead in Christ shall rise first." This refers to Christians that have died previously. It is a resurrection of their bodies to unite with their souls. Immediately following this event the Christians "who are alive and remain will be caught up together with them in the clouds to meet the Lord in the air."

In other words, if you are a true believer in Jesus Christ, and you are alive at the time of the Rapture, you will bypass death. You will be instantly changed. You will have a glorified body as Jesus had after His resurrection.

Another Bible reference concerning the Rapture is found in I Corinthians 15:51-52. It says: "Behold, I tell you a mystery; we shall not all sleep, but we shall all be changed, in a moment, in the twinkling of an eye, at the last trumpet; for the trumpet will sound, and the dead will be raised imperishable, and we shall be changed."

Four points from this reference explain the Rapture:
1. "Behold, I tell you a mystery." A mystery is a secret in the mind of God, as revealed through Paul. This word is used when referring to the Church Age in Ephesians 3:1-7; Romans 16:25-27; and Colossians 1:26-29.
2. "We shall not all sleep." We shall not all die. "Sleep" here is referring to the believer's death.
3. "But we shall all be changed." The Christian's body is transformed into a glorified body.
4. "In the twinkling of an eye." It happens instantly in a fraction of a second.

From these references we can conclude that: the "dead in Christ" are resurrected first; there is a generation of Christians who will not die; it is a mystery; the Christians who are alive will have their bodies transformed; this generation of believers will go to be with Jesus Christ; and it will happen instantaneously.

In practical terms let's look at how things may appear when the Rapture happens. Let's suppose you are not a Christian but your spouse is a believer.

You are taking your wife out to eat one Friday night. As you drive to your favorite restaurant, she disappears, vanishes from the car. She is there one minute and gone the next. You are shocked to put it mildly. Maybe it's a dream, you figure, some type of mental dysfunction, or a brain chemistry imbalance.

Immediately following her disappearance you hear crashing sounds of auto accidents and then come the police and ambulance sirens. Your favorite radio station interrupts the regular programming with an urgent news announcement. A newscaster stutters as he tries to report the disappearances of large numbers of people and numerous accidents. You detect the sheer terror in his voice as it matches your own racing heartbeat.

You mentally review all the possible explanations you can dream up, but none of your worst case scenarios seem to fit. As you turn around to go back home, you hear a report on the radio that graves have been opened, and body remains and skeletons have vanished.

What does this all mean? Then you remember some of the things you have been reading by the New Age authors. It made so much sense to you. You recall how your wife seemed so narrow-minded about her Christian beliefs. You couldn't understand why she spent so much time reading the Bible, going to church, praying and talking about the Lord. You sure loved her but her interest in Christianity bored you to tears. It's the one area the two of you did not have in common and did not discuss.

Over the last couple of years you have read fascinating material from the New Age authors about how the world was created and mankind came into being. You also read their predictions about the future. It is then you begin to think back on some of their predictions. What they said is now beginning to make sense. You decide to start looking for answers. In your search you decide to look back over those New Age predictions. It never occurs to you that the Bible could explain the recent traumatic events. After all, the Bible is outdated and archaic, but New Age material is up to date. Driving carefully to avoid the traffic accidents and the hysterical people milling in the streets, you go home to begin your search.

THE "NEW AGE RAPTURE"

Previously we reviewed media deception. More and more, as man becomes oriented toward a world that is ruled by Satan, he moves farther away from God's truths as set forth in His Word.

The man in our story goes through a desensitization process much the same way a cold-blooded animal can be slowly boiled to death. He becomes like his environment until it is too late.

As God permits, the world is temporarily under Satan's power and he has power over it (I John 5:19). As Satan deceives mankind through the media, culture, and literature, mankind is set up to believe a lie. The ones that hear the gospel and yet do not receive it (harden themselves toward God), God in turn sends a "deluding influence so that they might believe what is false" (II Thessalonians 2:11 NASB)

Let's look at what form this delusion may take. We have looked at the UFO cover-up by the government for national security reasons. We have also looked at the Federal Emergency Management Agency (FEMA) training manual and the section entitled "Enemy Attack and UFO Potential."

In order for a counterfeit gospel to stand up in the last days, it would have to provide an alternative explanation for the events that occur as a fulfillment of Bible prophecy.[252] The Star Trek mentality and "beam me up, Scotty," merely laid the groundwork for UFO's and alien encounters to provide a delusion for the remaining unbelievers after the Rapture occurs.

Second Thessalonians 2:3-10 discusses the apostasy (falling away from the truth) which is present now, the activity of the Antichrist, and the removal of the "restrainer" (Holy Spirit who indwells every believer). This occurs by way of the Rapture of the true church of Jesus Christ. In verse 11 of the same chapter it states, "And for this reason God will send upon them a deluding influence so that they might believe what is false."

In *Celestine Prophecy*, James Redfield states that everyone at some point "will vibrate highly enough so that we can walk into heaven, in our same form."[253] It is true that a rapture in our bodies will take place, but it does not include everyone. It only includes the true believers in Jesus Christ.

Many New Age prophets believe in a disappearance or rapture by way of UFO's. Barbara Hubbard, a New Age author, makes the following statement. "Those vehicles which you have called UFO's are moving in ultrahigh frequencies. They slow down to 'appear', and 'quicken to disappear.' You shall do the same, and shall be taken up in the fullness of time in those vehicles, in your quickened condition."[254] Of course to make this trip we have to be an ascended being, which requires a quickened being, which requires a quickened human, according to Hubbard. The definitions are vague.

When Christians disappear, what will the New Agers think? Will they think the wicked have been removed as some of their "prophecies" imply? Or will they think the Christians were beamed aboard a spaceship?

When the world is falling apart following the Rapture, will they look for salvation in a spaceship or in the God who formed the universe?[255] Or, will they look for a man who later claims to be God (II Thessalonians 2:4) (the Antichrist)?

It is interesting to note that many of the New Age prophets make their predictions according to messages they receive from spirits or guides. Ruth Montgomery, a well known New Age writer, has guides which speak through her.

She speaks of the earth going through an axis shift which will have catastrophic effects. The guides tell her that most people will remain on the planet to ride out the shift but some will be temporarily removed. She quotes her guides as saying the following: "'Now as to those being rescued,' they write, 'it will be a massive undertaking, but the space aliens, as you call them, will indeed be on hand to lift off some chosen earthlings who will remain in earth orbit until that planet settles back into proper rotation.'"[256]

There will be a removal of people from the earth but they are the true believers in Jesus Christ. They will meet the Lord at the Rapture (I Thessalonians 4:16-17). They will not go into "orbit" for a temporary period of time.

According to Frank Stranges, Ph.D., author of *Stranger at the Pentagon*, there are certain events that will transpire in the last days. Stranges claims that he received this message directly from an alien in human form from another planet. His first three predictions are as follows:

1. "Millions will vanish from the face of the earth.
2. Children will be reported missing (remember the prediction that the space brothers will take our youngsters first), loved ones gone, graves opened.
3. Distress of nations, such as never before transpired on this planet."[257]

These predictions are very close to Bible prophecy with two critical exceptions. Stranges never specifies what group disappears in the vanishings. There is no reference to the disappearance of true believers in Jesus Christ. The other exception refers to the space brothers. There is no biblical confirmation of the "space brothers."

According to some New Age literature, the ET's are concerned that "Mother Earth" will destroy a majority of life as she attempts to "cleanse herself." In order to prevent this from happening, ET's have a plan to "remove, that is, evacuate the millions of people who are 'out of vibration' with Earth Mother! . . . When the global situation reaches a crisis point on Earth, they will evacuate these people in a 'twinkling of an eye,' then transfer them to larger ships for re-education and initiation into higher levels of consciousness!"[258]

Kay Wheeler, author of *Connecting Link* magazine, a quarterly New Age periodical, believes that people with thought patterns of the past will be the ones removed:

> Many of these beings who are leaving this planet at this time have completed that which they came to do. It is a time of great rejoicing for them. . . . Many beings must move on, for their thought patterns are of the past. They hold on to these thoughts that keep Earth held back.[259]

In researching the New Age prophetic literature, one of the more common beliefs involves the Rapture of a population with old-fashioned thinking patterns. This is often a reference to fundamental Christianity. This New Age belief concerning the Rapture is accurate. It will only involve the Christians, but they are not responsible for "keeping the earth held back."

The New Age literature puts an emphasis on an accelerating Mother Earth which needs to rid itself of the people who don't fit in. The trend is toward an evolving consciousness or a consciousness evolution.

In this consciousness evolution we have what one New Age author refers to as the "quantum instant." In Hubbard's words, "those of you who happen to be alive at the time of the actual quantum instant, will be changed while still alive. You will not have to undergo physical death or the reconstitution process."[260] She identifies the people who bypass death as the saints. This is true. When the word saint is used in the Bible, it refers to true believers in Christ. The author identifies saints as people who follow Jesus' example. Salvation is not following Jesus' example, it is believing that he died for your sins (John 3:16), and accepting Him into your heart (Revelation 3:20).

Missler and Eastman, Christian writers, conducted extensive research concerning messages from aliens. In *Alien Encounters*, they summarize alien messages:

> In the last several decades, dozens of contactees have delivered messages from alien entities which state that Earth changes are not the wrath of God; they are the birth pangs of our Earth Mother who is trying to expel the 'dark forces' from her surface so she can evolve to a higher dimension of existence.[261]

Quotes from New Age prophets concerning their belief in a rapture-type event, could continue at length, but the difference between a New Age rapture and the Biblical Rapture is clear.

Some people propose that the Biblical Rapture and the coming alien evacuation (new age rapture) are one and the same. They propose that the apostle Paul and Jesus were both describing a coming evacuation by extraterrestrials.[262]

Hopefully, the distinction between the two events has become clear. The prediction of an alien evacuation will very likely set the stage so the people who remain will "BELIEVE A LIE" (II Thessalonians 2:11).

On returning to our short story about the Rapture, what does our character believe now? After reviewing the New Age prophets we have quoted, he feels quite confident that he now understands the truth. While his wife was with him he "did not receive the love of the truth so as to be saved. And for this reason God will send upon them [him] a deluding influence so that they [he] might believe what is false" (II Thessalonians 2:10-11 NASB).

If you do not know Jesus Christ as your Lord and Savior, there is still time. You can say the following prayer:

> "Lord Jesus forgive me for my sins and come into my heart. Make me the kind of person you want me to be. Thank you for dying on the cross for my sins. Thank you for forgiving my sins and giving me eternal life."

If you say this prayer and it expresses the desire of your heart, Christ will come into your life as He promised. Revelation 3:20 says, "Behold, I stand at the door and knock; if any one hears My voice and opens the door, I will come in to him, and will dine with him, and he with Me."

If you prayed this prayer and it expressed your heart, you are now a born again Christian and will meet Jesus at the Rapture. If you are left behind after the Rapture, you can still be saved, but will have to endure a horrible tribulation period. This tribulation period is God's judgment on this earth. According to Jesus, "there will be a great tribulation, such as has not occurred since the beginning of the world until now, nor ever shall" (Matthew 24:21 NASB). You will not want to go through this tribulation period. This period is the topic of the next section.

In Chapter Six, we have reviewed UFO's, ET's, and the Rapture. The evidence for the existence of UFO's and ET's is extensive. Our review has taken us through three different ways of interpreting that evidence: scientific, New Age, and Biblical. The Rapture was viewed through both the New Age perspective and the Biblical perspective.

As we review our pyramid, the first five chapters dealt with prophecy, world views, and current events. Chapter Six began the future prophetic fulfillment and moves right into the tribulation period or the capstone of the pyramid found in our final chapter, The Apocalypse.

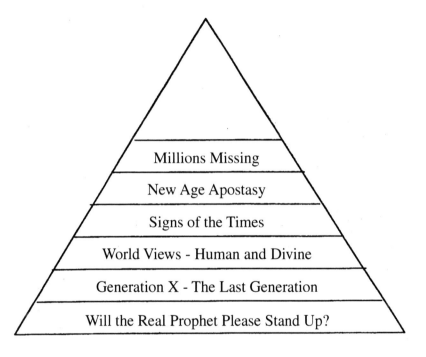

-SEVEN -

APOCALYPSE / LAST DAYS

"And unless those days had been cut short, no life would have been saved; but for the sake of the elect those days shall be cut short."
Matthew 24:22 NASB

This final chapter will cover the most horrifying days in the history of mankind. Beginning with a world in total shock following the Rapture of the Church (true believers in Jesus Christ), Chapter Seven will then proceed to cover some of the main events that will happen during this seven-year tribulation period.

RAPTURE SHOCK

In the days following the mass disappearance of millions of people, called the Rapture, the world will be in a state of chaos. An explanation for this event will be demanded as people desperately seek answers.

Satan and his hierarchy of fallen angels, working through human experts, will provide one or more explanations. The one world stage preceding the Rapture will be in place. One possible scenario preceding the Rapture is open alien contact. If this were to happen, it would cause a great "apostasy" to help explain away the Rapture.

As discussed in the previous section, abduction by aliens is a possible explanation. Satan has used the New Age philosophy and the New Age prophets to pave the way for the Rapture.

Although a number of other explanations may be given, the UFO abduction explanation appears more probable. The people left behind will be desperate for an explanation. The ones who have been exposed to the gospel and did not accept it will be spiritually blinded. They will believe a lie (II Thessalonians 2:10-11).

PENTECOST REVERSAL

When God dealt with the nation of Israel, there was a correlation between events, holy days, and number of years prophesied. The prophecies in the Old Testament were very specific in every way, including sequence of time.

For example, the prediction of Judah's 70 year captivity under Babylon was predicted in Jeremiah 25:11. It says, "and this whole land will be a desolation and a horror, and these nations shall serve the king of Babylon seventy years." Daniel referred back to Jeremiah near the end of the 70-year captivity. He knew when the end of the captivity was (Daniel 9:2). The exact number of years was predicted.

Another example is the 70 weeks prophecy in Daniel 9:24-27, symbolizing or representing 490 years. There was an exact number of years decreed for the nation of Israel. The first segment of time was 69 weeks (483 years). The start was the decree under Artaxerxes to rebuild Jerusalem in 444 B.C. It ran until Messiah the Prince was "cut off" (crucified) in 33 A.D. The remaining one week (seven years) is the tribulation period.

Jesus died during Passover which was in observance of the Israelites being freed from Egypt. The final plague before the Egyptians freed the Israelites was the death of the first born in each family. The Israelites were protected or passed over by the death angel if the blood of a lamb was applied to the doorposts (Exodus 12:21-23). Jesus' death occurred simultaneously with the celebration of that event. He was the ultimate sacrificial lamb. His crucifixion could have occurred at any time during the year, but God chose the Passover celebration.

If God deals in an exact, specific way with Israel regarding numbers of years and parallel events, like the Passover and the crucifixion of Christ, would He deal in a similar manner concerning the church? The day of Pentecost was a Jewish holiday that occurs 50 days after the Passover.

The first day of Pentecost following the death of our Lord (at Passover) was the start of the Christian Church. This event was marked by the outpouring of the Holy Spirit (Acts 2:1-21). The Holy Spirit now indwells every believer in Jesus Christ (Ephesians 1:13-14; 4:30; Romans 8:9).

When the Rapture occurs, Christians "meet the Lord in the air . . ." (I Thessalonians 4:17). The believers, who are indwelt by the Holy Spirit, ascend to join Jesus Christ. The Church, composed of believers (Ephesians 5:25-32), will meet the Lord in the air.

The Church was established by the outpouring of the Holy Spirit (Acts 2: 1-4). The Church is raptured (I Thessalonians 4:16-17) and the Holy Spirit is removed from the earth (II Thessalonians 2:7). We have, in essence, a reversal of Pentecost.

There is also another parallel to note. On the "Calendar in Israel" in the Bible Knowledge Commentary by Walvoord and Zuck, Pentecost comes sometime during May or June.[263] The calendar parallels "Pentecost" with "early figs ripen."

Matthew 24:32 relays the parable of the fig tree, ". . . When its branch has already become tender, and puts forth its leaves you know that summer is near." As mentioned in Chapter 2, the fig tree symbolizes Israel. Putting forth its leaves immediately before it ripens signifies that the return of Christ is near the time Israel becomes a nation (1948). Verse 34 continues, ". . . This generation will not pass away until all these things take place."

Let's briefly review the parallels for the Church. Israel is symbolized by a fig tree. The putting forth of its leaves in the spring signifies the closeness of summer (Matthew 24:32), which is when the fig tree ripens. Pentecost was in the summer when the fig tree ripens. Could the Rapture happen at the time of Pentecost (May –

June) in a year not too far away? Or at the feast of trumpets in the late summer or early fall? Perhaps even this year? It is something to consider! Another name on the Jewish calendar for Pentecost was First Fruits.

OVERVIEW OF THE AGES

In order to see the tribulation period in its historical context, we will quickly review historical world empires and prophetic time periods. The historical world empires known as the "Times of the Gentiles" are found in Chapter 2. The 70 weeks in Daniel is a prophecy concerning Israel's time line, found in Chapter 1.

Times of the Gentiles - Began in 606 B.C. with the Captivity of Judah

Chapter 2 of Daniel describes King Nebuchadnezzar's dream of an image in which Daniel told the dream and gave the interpretation. The dream represented four world empires.

The first empire was the Babylonian Empire which was the head made of gold. It began in 626 B.C. The second empire was the Medo-Persian Empire represented by the chest and arms made of silver. It began in 539 B.C. The third empire was Greece, represented by the belly and thighs made of bronze, which began in 330 B.C. The fourth empire was the Roman Empire represented by the legs of iron and feet of iron and clay, which began its rise in 242 B.C.

Jerusalem later fell in 63 B.C. Three of the four empires were overtaken by the succeeding empires, except for Rome. The two iron legs represented the divided Roman Empire. The capital of the Eastern Roman Empire was Constantinople. Rome was the capital of the Western Roman Empire. "Rome held sway when Jesus was born in Bethlehem and when He was crucified."[264]

The feet and toes are made of iron like the legs but the iron is mixed with clay. The ten toes in Daniel 2:40-43 parallel the ten horns in Daniel 7:7 and Revelation 13:1; they are identified as "ten kings" in Daniel 7:24.

We know that the ten toes represent a revived Roman Empire because the final Roman Empire with ten kings has never been destroyed. It has yet to be established. **"There has never been a period in the Roman Empire when ten kings have sat simultaneously."**[265]

"By the time Christ was born, all of western Asia, northern Africa, southern Europe, including a portion of Great Britain, had succumbed to Rome. . . ."[266] When looking to a future revived Roman Empire, it would cover the same geographical areas as in Jesus' day.

As discussed in a previous chapter, the Church Age was a mystery and was not revealed in the Old Testament. Some of the Old Testament prophecies included both comings of Christ in the same verse. The Church Age is sometimes referred to as a "parenthesis."

An example of an Old Testament prophecy referring to both comings of Christ in the same verse, yet not mentioning the Church Age, is found in Isaiah 61:2, where "the expression 'to proclaim the year of the Lord's favor' is immediately followed by 'and the day of vengeance of our God.' The 'year of the Lord's favor' refers to the first coming of Christ, and the 'day of vengeance,' to his second. When quoting this verse in the synagogue at Nazareth (Luke 4:16-21), Christ stopped in the middle of the verse at the end of the description of his first coming."[267] The second half of the verse refers to His Second Coming.

Israel's Clock - Daniel's 70 Weeks Prophecy

The "70 weeks" prophecy is found in Daniel 9:24-27. In contrast to "Times of the Gentiles," which referred to succeeding world empires, this prophecy refers to a Jewish time line by way of Jewish years (360 days).

This prophecy is specifically to the Jewish people and the nation of Israel. "Seventy weeks have been decreed for your people and your holy city . . ." (Daniel 9:24 NASB). The Angel Gabriel was speaking to Daniel. The reference to "your people" and "your holy city" is a reference to the Israelites and Jerusalem.

Seventy weeks represents 490 years (for an explanation of the interpretation of "weeks," see Chapter 1, "Daniel's 70 weeks"). The Jewish time clock started at the "decree to restore and rebuild Jerusalem" (Daniel 9:25 NASB). The decree to restore and rebuild Jerusalem was issued under Artaxerxes in 444 B.C.

After 69 weeks, the Messiah will be "cut off" (Daniel 9:25-26) or crucified. Sixty nine weeks represents 483 years of the 490 year prophecy.

The remaining one week or seven years represents the tribulation period. The church age is between the end of the 483 years (the crucifixion) and the start of the tribulation period.

Prophetic Clocks

The Lord deals with Israel and the church differently. "It seems that the Lord deals with Israel and the Church mutually exclusively. A chess clock, with its two interlocked representations, is an illustrative example; one clock is stopped while the other is running."[268]

Prophetically, Israel was given precise prophecies by way of a succession of world empires or predictions in terms of years (70 years captivity in Jeremiah and 70 weeks in Daniel). The Church is given signs preceding the Second Coming (Matthew 24; Mark 13; Luke 21) but not an exact date. Matthew 24:36 says, "But of that day and hour no one knows . . . but the Father alone."

In regards to the Church Age, Dwight Pentecost states: "The concept must stand that this whole age with its program was not revealed in the Old Testament, but constitutes a new program and new line of revelation in this present age."[269] In many ways Biblical prophecy in the church age is like a puzzle. The pieces of the puzzle include the signs preceding the Second Coming coupled with current events. As the time gets closer, the picture nears completion.

Time Gap

According to Scripture, we know the start of the Church Age began at Pentecost. We know the consummation of the Church Age occurs at the Rapture. We also know what event restarts Israel's prophetic clock: a covenant between Israel and the Antichrist (Daniel 9:27). This starts the seven-year tribulation period also known as Daniel's seventieth week.

What the Bible doesn't reveal is the interlude between the Rapture and the beginning of the tribulation period. One misconception concerning the pre-tribulation Rapture is that it begins the tribulation period. The beginning of the tribulation period is marked by the signing of the covenant between Israel and the Antichrist. We are not given the time period between the Rapture and the signing of the covenant.[270]

The Rapture will occur prior to the beginning of the tribulation period. In reference to the Antichrist, the Bible says he is being "restrained." Second Thessalonians 2:7-8 says, ". . . He who now restrains will do so until he is taken out of the way, and then that lawless one will be revealed. . . ."

The only thing restraining the Antichrist, or having the power to restrain the Antichrist, is the Holy Spirit who will be "taken out of the way" when the Rapture occurs. Following the Rapture, the Antichrist will be revealed. There are some scholars who believe that the Rapture happens in the middle of the tribulation period, prior to the Great Tribulation (last three and one-half years). Whether the correct interpretation of Scripture is pre-tribulation Rapture (prior to the seven year start) or mid-tribulation, it will happen prior to the horrible judgments which occur in the last half of the tribulation (Great Tribulation) period.

"There is some passage of time between the revelation of antichrist and the beginning of the tribulation period. . . . 'Rome wasn't built in a day.' It was true in ancient times. It will also apply to the revived Roman Empire under antichrist."[271]

Most likely a global disturbance of some type (war, environmental destruction, Rapture) will pave the way for the Antichrist to sign a peace plan (Daniel 9:27). Other causes are also possible. For example, terrorism, the threat of war, and pressure by allies, have led to peace treaty negotiations between Israel and Palestine, and between Israel and Syria, during the late 1990's and into the year 2000. It is possible that these are preliminary to the seven-year peace covenant to be signed by Israel and the Antichrist.

The first half of the tribulation will most likely be characterized by peace, at least in comparison to the second half known as the "Great Tribulation." The Bible says, "While they are saying 'peace and safety!' then destruction will come upon them suddenly like birth pangs upon a woman with child; and they shall not escape" (I Thessalonians 5:3 NASB).

Right at the Door

How close is mankind to the final seven year count down known as the tribulation period? Very close! We cannot know the day or the hour (Matthew 24:36), but we are given enough signs to know the season.

The three remaining elements of the last days are the **global economy**, the **global government**, and the **global religion**.[272] Israel became a nation in 1948. **Within one generation of that point in time, the three remaining elements will happen.** In Chapter 4, we reviewed the formation of these three elements, particularly the movement toward a one world religion.

The three global elements of economy, government and religion do not have to be established prior to the Rapture, but will be in place during the tribulation period. Mankind is moving toward a one world unification.

Prior to 1945, the Book of Revelation was just symbolic. After 1945, the results of a nuclear holocaust could be envisioned. Sixty years ago, the descriptions in the Apocalypse were beyond comprehension. It could not be envisioned, apart from a supernatural intervention.[273]

Throughout the history of the Church, up until 40 – 50 years ago, the book of Revelation could not be understood. It was a mysterious book of symbols. Daniel received and recorded a revelation about the end times (Daniel 12). Daniel responded to this revelation; he said, "as for me, I heard but could not understand; so I said, 'my Lord, what will be the outcome of these events?' and he said, 'go your way, Daniel, for these words are concealed and sealed up until the end time" (Daniel 12:8).

John recorded his vision in the Book of Revelation. He used the words that were common in his day for describing events that were revealed to him. Planes, helicopters, guns, and bombs were unknown in John's day. He described what he saw as a time traveler. "John was a 1st century man trying to describe a 21st century war."[274]

Our current generation is the only generation since the time of Christ capable of fulfilling one of the prophecies found in Revelation 9:16. This refers to the number of soldiers invading Israel from the east (China). "And the number of the armies of the horsemen was two hundred million . . ." (Revelation 9:16 NASB). Commenting on this prophecy, Hal Lindsay states:

> When John made the prophecy of 200 million Asian solders invading Israel to take on the armies of the west, which will be led by the revived Roman Empire, there were not 200 million people in the world. China can now raise an army of 352 million soldiers. [275]

Only in this generation, since Israel became a nation, are we able to understand prophecy. Daniel 12:9 has come true: ". . . these words are concealed and sealed up until the end time." What was concealed is now being revealed in these last days.

The first three chapters of Revelation cover the Church Age. According to Dwight Pentecost, "Chapters 1-3 present the development of the church in this present age."[276] The remainder of the Book of Revelation never mentions the word "church." Chapter 6 begins the tribulation period which concludes in chapter 19. Chapter 3 concludes with one last invitation to people prior to the Rapture. "Behold I stand at the door and knock; if anyone hears My voice and opens the door, I will come into him and dine with him, and he with Me." (Revelation 3:20 NASB).

THE LONGEST SEVEN YEARS IN HISTORY: THE TRIBULATION PERIOD

The tribulation period has been referred to as Jacob's trouble (Jeremiah 30:5-7) and the day of the Lord (I Thessalonians 5:2). This seven-year time period is a judgment on the whole world.

Israel's prophetic time clock begins when the Antichrist signs a peace agreement with Israel (Daniel 9:27). God has turned His attention back to Israel as the 70th week of Daniel or the seven-year tribulation countdown begins.

Character Line Up

There are several characters who play major roles during this period of time. Let's review some of these people and their characteristics.

Antichrist

This is the key player and Satan's right-hand man. Scripture gives him three common names:
1. Antichrist (I John 2:18)
2. Man of lawlessness (II Thessalonians 2:3, 8)
3. Beast (Revelation 13:1, 17-18; Daniel 7:19).

-- Out of the Sea

The Antichrist comes out of the gentile nations and is a gentile leader. Revelation 13:1 says: "and I saw a beast coming up out of the sea, having ten horns. . . ." "John sees this beast coming up 'out of the sea.'. . . John didn't call it a beast because it was a Gentile. It comes up out of the sea of nations. In Daniel Chapter 7, the prophet records a dream that he had in which he saw the rise and fall of four gentile world empires. Each was characterized as a beast coming from the sea of nations"[277] (See Daniel 7:1-7).

-- Man of Sin

In II Thessalonians 2:3, the Antichrist is described as the man of sin, ". . . the son of perdition." This man is evil to the core. The Antichrist will be characterized as follows.

Daniel 7
1. He will utter great boasts (verse 8).
2. He will persecute and wage war against Christians (verse 21).
3. He will make changes in time and in the law (verse 25).
4. He will be destroyed forever (verse 26).

Daniel 11
1. He will "exalt" himself against every god (verse 36).
2. He will speak "monstrous" things against the "God of gods" (verse 36).
3. He relies on his military strength (verse 38).
4. He is a merciless conqueror (verses 39 - 42).
5. He will "gain control" over the world's economy (verse 43).
6. He will come to his end between "the seas and the beautiful Holy Mountain" (verse 45).[278]

Revelation 13
1. He is arrogant and blasphemous (verse 5-6).
2. He wars against the saints (verse 7).
3. He demands worship or imposes death on non-worshipers (verse 15).

Other references:
1. He is a covenant-breaker (Daniel 9:27).
2. He is a "man of lawlessness" (II Thessalonians 2:3).

In addition to the above, the Antichrist will be head over the revived Roman Empire consisting of ten nations (Daniel 2:40-43; 7:23-24).

False Prophet: Looks like a Lamb, Talks like a Dragon

The false prophet is the Antichrist's right-hand man. Revelation 13:11 describes the false prophet as "another beast." "And I saw another beast coming up out of the earth; and he had two horns like a lamb, and he spoke as a dragon" (Revelation 13:11 NASB).

He is described as a "beast" and a "lamb with two horns." He is also referred to as the "false prophet" (Revelation 16:13; 19:20; 20:10).

-- Out of the Earth

The false prophet comes "out of the earth" (Revelation 13:11), whereas the Antichrist comes "out of the sea" (Revelation 13:1). The sea of nations is a reference to the whole earth or the gentile nations. The word "earth" (land) is representative of Israel. The word "land" "with the definite article and not otherwise defined always refers to Israel."[279]

The false prophet will probably be a Jew, according to some commentators. He is described as a "lamb" who points the way to the first beast, the Antichrist (Revelation 13:12).

-- The Man Behind the Man

The role of the false prophet is to "make the earth and those who dwell in it to worship the first beast . . ." (Revelation 13:12 NASB). Just as the Antichrist has a role that is more political in nature, the false prophet has a more religious role. It could be paralleled to the Holy Spirit's role in pointing Christians toward Jesus. The false prophet derives power and authority from both Satan (dragon) and the Antichrist (Revelation 13:4, 12). He has the ability to perform great signs and miracles (verse 13), and "he deceives those who dwell on the earth because of the signs . . ." (Revelation 13:14 NASB).

-- Miracles and Images

The false prophet has the power to perform miracles and great signs, "so that he even makes fire come down out of heaven to the earth in the presence of men" (Revelation 13:13 NASB). He is empowered by Satan along with the Antichrist.

During the tribulation period, the Antichrist is slain and then brought back to life (Revelation 13:3). As a result of this miracle, the whole earth follows after him. This occurs around the middle of the tribulation period.

Through Satan's power, the Antichrist is brought back to life. It is questionable whether Satan has that kind of power or whether a great deception will be involved.

In Chapter 6, we discussed aliens and "their incredible mastery over the laws of physics and the seemingly supernatural powers they possess. The ability to perform 'signs and wonders' and provide answers for mankind's problems are characteristics shared by the Antichrist as well. He will have a global plan that is so incredible that he will be embraced as a technological savior."[280]

As Christ died and was resurrected, so the great counterfeiter, the Antichrist, will be or will appear to be slain and resurrected. Jesus' death and resurrection are the foundation stone for Christianity. The Antichrist's death and resurrection (whether real or through supernatural deception) establishes or gives power to the false world religion. "... and the whole earth was amazed and followed after the beast" (Revelation 13:3 NASB).

In consideration of the supernatural characteristics of the Antichrist, where will he say he got his power? If he says God, he would be rejected by the secular scientific community. If he says from demonic forces, he also would be rejected by many. Contemporary Christian authors, Missler and Eastman, "believe that it is very likely that the coming world leader will boast of a connection with the powerful god-like alien entities who have, it is believed, overcome the problems of poverty, famine, disease, war, and the pain of cultural and religious division."[281]

The whole UFO – alien belief system that has been established will very likely come into the picture. If UFO's are the delusion or the false explanation for the Rapture, the people left behind will have a belief system that paves the way for the Antichrist.

The false prophet points the way to the Antichrist. He makes an image of the Antichrist who has come back to life (Revelation 13:14 NASB). He is given the power to give life to the image and gives it the power to speak. He requires worship of the image and death to those who refuse (Revelation 13:15).

Remember Daniel, Chapter 3? Nebuchadnezzar made an extremely large golden image of himself and required everyone to worship it (Daniel 3: 1-6). He made the same requirements, death to those who refuse to worship.

An interesting parallel can be drawn between these passages. During the Babylonian empire, a great image of the king was made with a mandatory worship requirement. During the tribulation, the world ruler, the Antichrist, does the same thing. The Babylonian empire was characterized by the occult (Daniel 2:2). The new world religion will be characterized by the occult (Revelation 9:20 – 21).

The only difference is the nature of the images built for worship. The false prophet gives life to the image. What does this mean? How can life be given to an inanimate object? How can the whole world worship it?

According to the Lalonde's book, *2000 A.D.*, it is a very high tech image. They believe the use of television can provide one way communication of the image to the whole world. They suggest that the image may exist only in cyberspace and there may be a way for the image electronically to know if everyone is worshiping it or not.[282]

The Good Guys: the Two Witnesses

Two men from God, His witnesses, come on the scene. "And I will grant authority to my two witnesses, and they will prophesy for twelve hundred and sixty days, clothed in sackcloth" (Revelations 11:3 NASB).

No one knows the exact identity of the two witnesses. Some authors believe "that they are Moses and Elijah, because of the similarity of judgment inflicted to those pronounced by Elijah and Moses, namely fire from heaven, turning water into blood, and smiting the earth with plagues."[283]

They prophesy for the last three and one-half years. They have the power to project fire to destroy anyone trying to harm them (Revelation 11:5). They have the power to stop rain like Elijah and to turn water into blood like Moses (verse 6).

These two witnesses have the following characteristics:
- They are sent by God to prophesy (Revelation 11:3)
- The period of time they prophesy is for three and one-half years (verse 3)

- They are most likely prophets of doom prophesying the coming of Jesus and God's judgment. They wear sackcloth like John the Baptist (verse 3)
- They have supernatural powers (verse 5)
- They are immune from death until their mission is accomplished (verse 7)
- They are killed by the Antichrist after their mission is accomplished (verse 7)
- Their bodies will be in the streets of Jerusalem for three and a half days (verses 8-9)
- People will rejoice over their death (verse 10)
- They are resurrected by God after three and a half days (verse 11) and
- They ascend into heaven (verse 12).

These two witnesses have supernatural powers from God. There is a display of the miraculous. They can project fire, turn water into blood, and smite the earth with every plague (Revelation 11:6).

We have seen Satan's powers in performing miracles though the Antichrist and the false prophet. Through the two witnesses, God's miraculous power is exhibited. It is similar to the display of miracles when Moses led the Israelites out of Egypt. Both Moses and the sorcerers produced miracles (Exodus 7:10-12). "...Aaron's staff swallowed up their staffs" (verse 12). God delivered Israel from Egypt and He will once again turn His attention to Israel. Romans 11:1 says, "I say then, God has not rejected Israel, has He? May it never be!"

God sent his two witnesses to prophesy in the interlude between the sixth and seventh trumpet judgment. His representatives are sent just prior to the most horrible judgments of mankind, the bowl judgments.

A Multitude of Jewish Evangelists: Sealing of 144,000 Jews for Jesus

As the world enters into a time of horrendous judgment, God appoints and seals 12,000 Jews from each of the twelve tribes of Israel (Revelation 7:3-8). No one knows the exact time within the seven year tribulation period that God seals His "bond servants." It is apparently before the time of the Great Tribulation (last three and one-half years). Revelation 7:2-3 says, "And I saw another angel ascending from the rising of the sun, having the seal of the living God; and he cried out with a loud voice to the four angels to whom it was granted to harm the earth and sea, saying, 'Do not harm the earth or sea or the trees, until we have sealed the bond-servants of our God on their foreheads.'"

According to Mark 13:10, "... the gospel must first be preached to all the nations." Many prophecy scholars expect the world-wide spread of the gospel to occur during the tribulation.[284]

These Jewish evangelists will spread the gospel across the globe. This will truly be a "Jews for Jesus" revival like the world has never seen.

This seal of the 144,000 Jews happens in the interlude between the sixth and seventh seal judgments. The Lord seals His representatives just prior to the trumpet judgments.

Due to modern means of communication, the gospel can be spread much quicker and can reach more people than ever before. An example is one of Billy Graham's last messages. "It was carried to more countries simultaneously by video than ever before. One reporter estimated that the evangelist preached the gospel that day to 281 million people. Even if that estimate was half right, that is an astonishing number."[285]

ON THE STARTING BLOCK

God's time clock is precise. He allotted 490 years (70 x 7) according to the 70 week prophecy of Daniel 9:24-27 (See Chapter

1 – Daniel's 70 weeks). The first 483 years took us from 444 B.C. to the crucifixion.

At the time of Jesus' crucifixion, Israel's clock stopped. Upon Jesus' triumphal entry into Jerusalem, ". . . He saw the city and wept over it, saying if you had known in this day, even you, the things which make for peace! But now they have been hidden from your eyes" (Luke 19:41-42 NASB).

The nation of Israel as a whole experienced a partial spiritual blindness (Romans 11:8) until the "fullness of the Gentiles have come in" (Romans 11:25 NASB) or until the Rapture. Israel was set aside for rejecting their Messiah, but Israel has not been rejected (Romans 11).

This interlude or parenthesis in Israel's time clock lasts from the crucifixion to the beginning of the tribulation. The tribulation period starts Israel's prophetic clock.

This prophetic clock, that stopped after 483 years on the 69th week in Daniel 9:26, will restart when the Antichrist signs a peace covenant with Israel for the final seven years or 70th week (Daniel 9:27).

The tribulation period is divided into 21 judgments: seven seal judgments, seven trumpet judgments, and seven bowl judgments. Each succeeding judgment is more destructive than the one before.[286]

We are close to the time of the Rapture which will open the door for the tribulation period. "Zola Levitt put it beautifully in a television broadcast. He said, 'We are pushing out the membrane of time that separates the Church Age from the beginning of the Tribulation.'"[287]

One White Horse / One "Bad News" Rider

The first seal is opened, "And I looked, and behold a white horse, and he who sat on it had a bow, and a crown was given to him; and he went out conquering and to conquer" (Revelation 6:2 NASB).

Riders of white horses usually symbolize victory. Christ rides a white horse at the Second Coming. The first seal symbolizes the beginning of the tribulation - not the end.

According to Walvoord and Zuck, "This ruler has a bow without an arrow, indicating that the world government which he establishes is accomplished without warfare."[288] The Church is gone. Satan's counterfeit Christ comes on the scene.

The Antichrist signs the covenant with Israel (Daniel 9:27) and symbolically rides in on a white horse. He is the counterfeit Christ. The restraining influence of the Holy Spirit through the Church is gone. The deception begins!

The Ultimate Politician

If you haven't previously trusted politicians, now is not the time to start. This man is no fool. He has the ability and charisma to put to shame the most loved and adored leaders throughout history.

The Antichrist gains the world's adoration by bringing peace to the earth during the first half of the tribulation period. Riding a white horse is the symbol of a conqueror.[289] According to the original Hebrew text, Daniel predicted, "And by means of peace, he will destroy many. . . ."[290]

The three and a half years preceding the Great Tribulation will be characterized as a relative time of peace.[291] Israel is at peace and feels secure as a result of the signed covenant with the Antichrist. Israel is referred to in Ezekiel 38:10 as a "land of unwalled villages." Another reference that characterizes the tribulation period during the first half is found in I Thessalonians, which states: "While they are saying, 'peace and safety!' then destruction will come upon them suddenly like birth pangs upon a woman with child; and they shall not escape" (I Thessalonians 5:3 NASB). This is a reference to the world just prior to the Great Tribulation when the trumpet and bowl judgments begin.

The Antichrist is conquering nations through this period of time without war but with the threat of war, as symbolized by a bow but no arrow. This bow could very likely be the threat of nuclear war. As leader of a ten nation revived Roman Empire, he would have a nuclear arsenal at his disposal that would intimidate any other nation. Besides, he is a man of peace. He walks softly but carries a big stick. "The crown identifies him as one who will eventually be accepted as king of the world."[292]

A TEMPLE REBUILT

A Jewish temple has to be rebuilt in Jerusalem in order for the Antichrist to desecrate the temple halfway through the tribulation period. Temple sacrifices will resume (Daniel 9:27).

The existence of a Jewish temple is further confirmed in Revelation 11:1-2 which states: "Rise and measure the temple of God, and the altar, and those who worship in it. . . . for it has been given to the nations; and they will tread under foot the holy city for forty-two months."

Prophecy teachers who interpret Scripture literally agree that a Jewish temple in Israel must be rebuilt. Historically, Israel has had two temples.

The first temple was built under Solomon and destroyed by the Babylonians in 586 B.C. The second temple began in 535 B.C. and was completed in 516 B.C. It was renovated by Herod the Great starting in 19 B.C. and finally destroyed by the Romans in 70 A.D. "That there will be a third temple is predicted by the prophet Daniel, the apostles Paul and John, and none other than the Lord Jesus Himself"[293] (Daniel 9:27; Matthew 24:15; II Thessalonians 2:3-4; Revelation 11:1-2).

Currently Gershom Solomon heads the Temple Mount Faithful movement, an organization dedicated to rebuilding the Temple. This is a man who definitely believes in a coming Messiah.

That Messiah is coming back. His name is Jesus Christ. He is first preceded by a counterfeit messiah, the Antichrist who desecrates the temple in the middle of the tribulation period and breaks his covenant with Israel (Daniel 9:27).

Solomon is not the only individual who is actively pursuing a rebuilt temple. "Many plans are being made for a rebuilt temple and many diverse groups in Israel are preparing for it."[294]

According to Bible prophecy, this temple will be in place during the tribulation period. The nation of Israel will have their temple for the first time since 70 A.D.

It is this temple that the Antichrist desecrates. He seats himself in the temple and displays himself as being God. He blasphemes God, builds an image of himself to be worshiped and breaks his covenant with Israel (II Thessalonians 2:4; Revelation 13:6; Daniel 9:27).

THE OTHER SIDE OF THE CURTAIN: A SUPERNATURAL WAR

Good and evil have a preliminary showdown. "And there was war in heaven, Michael and his angels waging war with the dragon. And the dragon and his angels waged war, and they were not strong enough, and there was no longer a place found for them in heaven. And the great dragon was thrown down, the serpent of old who is called the devil and Satan, who deceives the whole world; he was thrown down to the earth, and his angels were thrown down with him" (Revelation 12:7-9 NASB).

This battle is fought in heaven. It is not the final battle of the tribulation period, which will occur at the Second Coming of Christ (Revelation 19).

This war in heaven sets the stage for the Great Tribulation period (final three and one-half years). "Here (Revelation 12:8-9) he will be cast out of heaven in the middle of the tribulation."[295] This will literally result in a hell on earth through wars and judgments.

Prior to this war in heaven, mankind has struggled or given into invisible supernatural demonic forces. The book of Ephesians states, "For our struggle is not against flesh and blood, but against the rulers, against the powers, against the world forces of this darkness, against the spiritual forces of wickedness in the heavenly places" (Ephesians 6:12 NASB). "The cosmic (spiritual) battle is going to become increasingly visible."[296]

THE UFO / ET CONNECTION

The previous chapter discussed UFO's, extraterrestrials, alien abductions, and hybrids. As stated earlier, there is a lot of documentation and evidence supporting the UFO/alien existence and their interaction with mankind.

The problem we run into is one of interpretation and the implications of the evidence obtained. The world view, the unbiblical view, generally supports the view that UFO's and ET's are a result of visitations from life on other planets. This world view disregards the Biblical view of a demonic deception.

The New Age begins when what was traditionally considered evil merges with the good. One key belief system of the New Age is "all is one" or "monism."[297]

With monism, we have the elimination of evil and the disregard of a dualistic world system that is built on a Biblical base of two kingdoms. One kingdom is God's and one is Satan's.

The Biblical world view puts aliens, UFO's, ET's, and abductions as coming from one of the two kingdoms. As pointed out earlier, the evidence points toward a demonic deception.

The natural human tendency is a desire to believe in UFO's as visitors from other planets (provided they're friendly). "As Pastor Joe Focht of Calvary Chapel of Philadelphia has said, 'If I wasn't a Christian, I'd probably believe we were placed on earth by aliens.' ... He says people want to believe in ancient astronauts, because it absolves them of their responsibility to their Creator. It gives them an out, and most people will take it every time."[298]

John Mack, a well-known psychiatrist who has done extensive research in the area of alien abduction and the hybridization program, makes the following statement:

> It is difficult to ignore the fact that the UFO abduction phenomenon is taking place . . . abductions seem to be concerned primarily with two related projects: changing human consciousness to prevent the destruction of the earth's life, and a joining of two species for the creation of a new evolutionary form.[299]

In light of our interpretation of Genesis 6:2, where the "sons of God" married the "daughters of men," as an interbreeding of fallen angels with humans, a hybridization program doesn't seem unrealistic. "John Mack, M.D., and other researchers believe that one of the primary purposes for the alleged alien abductions is the production of hybrid (half-alien, half-human) offspring."[300]

Hebrews 13:2 says, "Do not neglect to show hospitality to strangers, for by this some have entertained angels without knowing it." This is a reference to good angels who evidently appear as human beings. If we have entertained good angels without knowing it, isn't it also possible that we have had contact with fallen angels or hybrids without knowing it?

The result of the ungodly union of fallen angels with humans in Genesis 6:2 was a powerful hybrid offspring - the Nephilim - who corrupted, harassed, and even killed mankind. "Now at the end of the 20th century, we have the return of 'alien' entities with apparent supernatural powers."[301] Many Christians can accept the idea of a union between humans and fallen angels in Noah's day, but recoil at the thought of a reoccurrence today.[302]

When we look at Revelation 12:9, we see Satan and his fallen angels cast out of heaven and "cast into the earth." We know that the tribulation period, especially the last half, will be energized by Satan.

"As we approach the end times, the interest in extraterrestrial life and UFO phenomena has reached an all time high. The prevailing view that they are our highly evolved ancestors . . . has prepared the world to receive them as our technological saviors. . . . The stage is set for the worship and reverence of alien entities."[303] It is very likely that the "alien entities" or "space brothers" will be considered "gods" during the tribulation period.

Daniel is also relevant here. The image in Daniel 2 is prophetic of the "Times of the Gentiles." It covers history from the Babylonian Empire through the tribulation period. The ten toes represent ten kings (Daniel 2:40-42) which represents the revived Roman Empire as understood by many commentators.

When we consider aliens and hybrids in the end times, we find an interesting prophecy in Daniel in regards to the ten toes. "And in that you saw the iron mixed with common clay, they will combine with one another in the seed of men; but they will not adhere to one another, even as iron does not combine with pottery" (Daniel 2:43 NASB).

The switching to a personal pronoun, "they will combine with one another in the seed of men . . ." is extremely suggestive. Missler and Eastman give their interpretation of this passage. They ask the question, "What (or who) are combining with the seed of men? Who are the Non-seed?" They believe the significance of Daniel's passage is staggering. They view aliens, and the hybrid offspring of aliens, as part of a new world empire, one in which UFO incidents are part of a political agenda.[304]

In light of our discussion, what are the implications concerning the Antichrist? "A number of prominent Bible teachers - Hal Lindsey and Dave Hunt, as examples – have publicly stated their view is that this leader will either be an alien or he will boast of alien connections!"[305]

Paul's Epistle to Timothy becomes very relevant in the end times. "But the Spirit explicitly says that in later times some will fall away from the faith, paying attention to the deceitful spirits and doctrines of demons" (I Timothy 4:1 NASB).

A RED HORSE WARRIOR

The opening of the second seal reveals a red horse which represents war. Revelation 6:3-4 says, "And when he broke the second seal, I heard the second living creature saying, 'Come.' And another, a red horse, went out; and to him who sat on it, it was granted to take peace from the earth, and that men should slay one another; and a great sword was given to him."

This is a picture of political power with the rider as the world ruler.[306] This second seal opens a time of war. "While they are saying, 'peace and safety,' then destruction will come upon them suddenly like birth pangs upon a woman with child . . ." (I Thessalonians 5:3 NASB).

Broken Covenant

The first seal parallels the signing of a covenant between the Antichrist and Israel. The second seal shatters that covenant (Daniel 9:27; Revelation 6:3-4).

The man of peace who characterizes the first half of the tribulation period shows his true colors at mid-tribulation. He is a man of war, a covenant breaker, and a blasphemer. He is no longer "under cover." Satan uses him in a direct way.

The Russian Confederacy Invasion

This invasion of Israel most likely occurs at mid-tribulation with the opening of the second seal, a red horse of war. This occurs while Israel is at peace. Israel is characterized as "living securely" and as a land of "unwalled villages" (Ezekiel 38:8-11). This invasion is led by Russia. John Walvoord, a well-known theologian, author, and an expert in the area of Bible prophecy, describes the root words for modern day Russia.

The described military invasion is led by "Gog." "Gog" refers to a leader and "Magog" refers to the territory from which he comes. According to Genesis 10:2 and I Chronicles 1:5, Magog is one of Japheth's sons. Japheth's father was Noah. Gog is referred to as the "chief prince of Mesheck and Tubal" (Ezekiel 38:2). Chief prince is translated in the NASB as "prince of Rosh." Rosh is the root for "Russia." This seems to be the land referred to in Scripture as the land north of Israel. [307]

Gog refers to the leader of this invasion. Magog, as we have indicated, is a reference to what is modern-day Russia. The country of Russia will invade with an alliance or confederation of nations or regions. This confederacy, allied with Russia, according to Ezekiel 38:5-6, consists of: Persia, Cush, Put, Gomer, and Beth-togarmah from the far north with all its troops.

The current names for these nations or regions include: Iran (Persia); Black African Nations (Cush); North African nations such as Libya, Algeria, Tunisia, Morocco, Mauritania (Put); Turkey (Gomer); and people to the north of Caucasus Mountains and eastward (Beth-togarmah from the far north). This rather large confederation has one thing in common. They are primarily Islamic. Muslims regard Jerusalem as the third holiest site in Islam, and they detest the Jewish nation of Israel.

Russia and the Muslim Confederacy invade Israel during a time of peace. This invasion will most likely take place in the middle of the tribulation period.

At mid-tribulation the Antichrist sets himself up in the rebuilt Jewish temple and declares himself to be God. According to the book of Thessalonians, "He will oppose and will exalt himself over everything that is called God or is worshiped, so that he sets himself up in God's temple, proclaiming himself to be God" (II Thessalonians 2:4 NIV). He also stops temple sacrifices (Daniel 9:27). This event is called the "abomination that causes desolation" predicted by the prophet Daniel. "This will be the sign that immediately precedes the Russian-led Islamic invasion of Israel."[308]

When the Antichrist desecrates the temple and sets himself up to be worshiped, he is rejected by the Jews. The Antichrist breaks his peace covenant as the Russian-Muslim invasion begins.

Up until now, Israel had the protection and backing of the Antichrist and the European Confederation (revived Roman Empire). Once Russia and the Islamic nations detect a weak link in the chain, by way of the chaos in Israel over the desecration of their temple, they invade Israel (Ezekiel 38).

Prior to this Russian invasion, the Antichrist rules the western nations but not the world. There is an escalation in power from western leader to world leader (Revelation 13:7). How does this shift in power take place?

The Balance of Power: God's Strategy

Ezekiel 38-39 shows God's wrath against Russia. When Israel was freed from Egyptian captivity under the leadership of Moses, God hardened Pharaoh's heart to pursue the Israelites so God would be honored through Pharaoh (Exodus 14:4).

In a similar way, God uses the Russian leader (Gog) to come against Israel. "Thus says the Lord God, 'behold, I am against you, O Gog, prince of Rosh, Meshech, and Tubal, and I will turn you about, and put hooks into your jaws, and I will bring you out, and all your army, horses and horsemen . . . '" (Ezekiel 38:3-4 NASB). Ezekiel goes on to say in verse 16, "And you will come up against my people Israel like a cloud to cover the land. It will come about in the last days that I shall bring you against My land, in order that the nations may know Me when I shall be sanctified through you before their eyes, O Gog."

God brings Russia and its Muslim allies against His people, Israel, so the nations will know Him. This invasion arouses the fury and anger of God (Ezekiel 38:18).

The Lord will destroy most of Russia (Ezekiel 38:19-39:6). This is either done directly by supernatural means or indirectly through a nuclear exchange. The end result of Russia's destruction is summed up in Ezekiel 39:7, "And My holy name I shall make known in the midst of My people Israel; and I shall not let My holy name be profaned any more and the nations will know that I am the Lord, the Holy One in Israel."

The Vacuum: a Power Shift

The destruction of Russia will be so great that it will take seven months for the Israelites to finish burying the dead in order to cleanse the land (Ezekiel 39:12).

After Russia is overthrown, the Federated States of Europe under the Antichrist move into the vacuum, with the Antichrist assuming the role of world leader. "Then there will be one world government, one world religion (worship of the Antichrist), one world dictator with no competition from the 'King of the North.'"[309]

When Russia is destroyed, many Jews will turn to God. "And the house of Israel will know that I am the Lord their God from that day onward" (Ezekiel 39:22 NASB).

Russian Update

When reading chapter 38 of Ezekiel, we know that the Russian leader (Gog) will probably be a powerful military leader. In 1998 in *Planet Earth: The Final Chapter*, Hal Lindsey made the following statement: "There is every probability that the next president of Russia will be a military strongman who will be bent upon re-establishing Russia's former super-power status. . . . I believe that the military strongman must come before the events of Ezekiel take place."[310]

This has occurred quickly. On Friday, December 31, 1999, President Boris Yeltsin abruptly resigned and Prime Minister Vladimir Putin was his chosen successor according to the Dallas Morning News, January 1, 2000.

> After the announcement, Mr. Putin – a former spy who was named prime minister five months ago – took control of Russia's formidable nuclear arsenal and announced that there would be no change in the nation's foreign policy objectives.[311]
>
> After he launched the war on Chechnya after his August appointment as premier, his popularity soared among the public hungry for a strongman....
>
> With his law-and-order stance, Mr. Putin, a KGB spy for 16 years, seems less the heir to Mr. Yeltsin than to Mr. Primakov, another longtime KGB operative....[312]

Lindsey seems to have been right on target. Mr. Putin launched the war on Chechnya, he is considered a "strongman," he took control of Russia's nuclear arsenal, and he was formerly a spy and a KGB agent. Mr. Putin may very well be "Gog" of Ezekiel 38.

WAR, FAMINE, POVERTY

War takes a heavy toll. Nuclear war will most likely characterize the Great Tribulation period. The toll it will take on mankind is unimaginable. Jesus, in the gospel of Matthew, says, "For then there will be a great tribulation, such as has not occurred since the beginning of the world until now, nor ever shall" (Matthew 24:21 NASB).

Prior to 1945, the book of Revelation was just symbols. After 1945, the results of a nuclear holocaust could be envisioned. Calvin and Luther saw Revelation as a book of symbols and confusing images. Today, the things described in prophecy take on substance.[313]

The description of the destruction of Russia in Ezekiel 38:19-22 could be describing the effects of a nuclear explosion. Although God initiates the invasion of Israel and causes the destruction of Russia, He may accomplish this through Israel's neutron bomb. "The Israeli defense forces have highly developed battlefield nukes called 'neutron bombs.' They are nicknamed 'dial a nuke' in reference to the precision with which they can be programmed just before being deployed. . . . And they only destroy living flesh."[314]

The effects of the neutron bomb would match the description found in Zechariah 14:12. "Now this will be the plague with which the Lord will strike all the peoples who have gone to war against Jerusalem; their flesh will rot while they stand on their feet, and their eyes will rot in their sockets, and their tongue will rot in their mouth" (Zechariah 14:12 NASB). "It is a terrifying thing to fall into the hands of the living God" (Hebrews 10:31 NASB). How true God's Word is, as demonstrated during the Great Tribulation.

The Black Horse: Starvation and Poverty

The breaking of the third seal reveals a black horse. The rider has a pair of scales in his hands (Revelation 6:5). War, famine, and poverty have traditionally gone hand-in-hand. Revelation 6:6 says, "And I heard as it were a voice in the center of the four living creatures saying, 'a quart of wheat for a denarius, and three quarts of barley for a denarius; and do not harm the oil and wine." A denarius was equivalent to one day's wages for one person. Thus, a day's wages would only pay for your food for that day. This excludes other expenses and dependents. Inflation skyrockets; money loses its value.

The Pale Horse: Deadly Rider

"And when He broke the fourth seal, I heard the voice of the fourth living creature saying, 'Come.' And I looked and behold, an ashen horse; and he who sat on it had the name 'Death'; and Hades was following with him. And authority was given to them over a fourth of the earth, to kill with sword and with famine and with pestilence and by the wild beasts of the earth" (Revelation 6:7-8 NASB).

The fourth seal speaks of the death of the physical body. Hades speaks of the claim for the soul and spirit of men. Death and Hades in this passage refer to unbelievers. John sees a pale horse which, according to the Greek text, means pale green. The unveiling of the fourth seal reveals a universal destruction, one fourth of the population, as a result of war and famine. This follows as the Antichrist rises in power to dominate the world.[315]

FOUR HORSEMEN: AN OVERVIEW OF THE TRIBULATION PERIOD

The first four seals, which reveal the four horsemen, cover the whole tribulation period. When reviewing the judgments (seals, trumpets, and bowls), we cannot view them just in a consecutive manner.

They build on each other and overlap one other. For example, the second seal is the red horse representing war. This seal, meaning war, continues throughout the remainder of the tribulation period and coincides with the other judgments.

The judgments can be viewed simultaneously, consecutively, and telescopically. See Chart 7. For a detailed listing and description of the seal, trumpet, and bowl judgments with references, see Appendix B.

Blood of the Martyrs: Fifth Seal

"And when he broke the fifth seal, I saw underneath the altar the souls of those who had been slain because of the word of God, and because of the testimony which they had maintained; and they cried out with a loud voice saying, 'How long, O Lord, holy and true, wilt thou refrain from judging and avenging our blood on those who dwell on the earth?'" (Revelation 6:9-10 NASB).

The breaking of the fifth seal gives us a picture in heaven through John's eyes. It is a picture of the souls of the slain martyrs who died because of their faithfulness to the gospel of Jesus Christ.

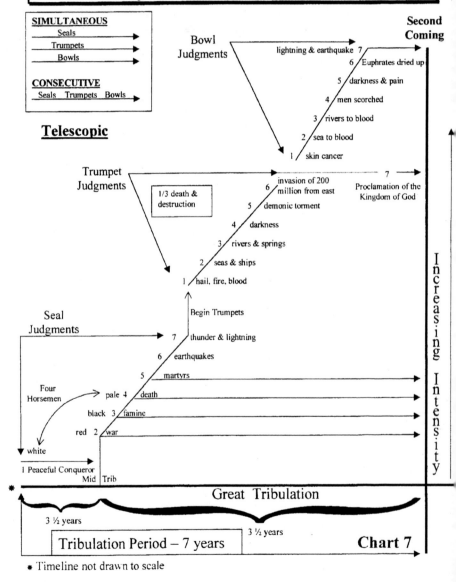

They ask, "How long . . . wilt thou refrain from judging and avenging our blood . . .?" "There comes a time when mercy has run its full course and God must execute judgment, so those people cry out that God might avenge them."[316]

The Antichrist engages in a mass killing of Christians. Everyone who accepts Christ during this period becomes the target of his fury.

Convulsions of Planet Earth: Sixth Seal

"And I looked when He broke the sixth seal, and there was a great earthquake; and the sun became black as sackcloth made of hair, and the whole moon became like blood. . . . And the sky was split like a scroll when it is rolled up; and every mountain and island were moved . . . and the commanders and the rich and the strong . . . said to the mountains and to the rocks, 'fall on us and hide us from the presence of Him who sits on the throne, and from the wrath of the Lamb'" (Revelation 6:12-16 NASB).

The opening of the sixth seal may signify a condition where world anarchy reigns.[317] This convulsing of the planet may also result from the Antichrist launching a nuclear counterattack against Russia and its Muslim allies. Revelation 6:14 says, "And the sky was split apart like a scroll." This is a description of the atmospheric effect from a nuclear blast.[318]

This sixth seal description reads like a hell on earth. This is not a good time to be alive. This span of time known as the Great Tribulation is mankind's worst nightmare!

If you don't know Jesus Christ as your Savior and Lord, now is the time to ask Him into your life. Do it now. Don't wait until after the Rapture. You may run out of time.

Ecological Horrors: Seventh Seal
- Trumpet Judgments

"And when He broke the seventh seal, there was a silence in heaven for about half an hour, and I saw the seven angels who stand before God; and seven trumpets were given to them.... And the first sounded, and there came hail and fire, mixed with blood, and they were thrown to the earth; and a third of the earth was burned up, and a third of the trees were burned up, and all the green grass was burnt up" (Revelation 8:1-7 NASB).

An ominous silence in heaven precedes the introduction of the trumpet judgments. The seventh seal introduces the trumpet judgments.

The trumpet judgments are sometimes referred to as the judgments of thirds. The earth is being systematically destroyed because of man's rebellious nature. He is unwilling to repent.

The scene of the seventh seal is in heaven. It is God's response to the prayers of the true believers in Jesus Christ. Revelation 8:4-5 says, "And the smoke of the incense, with prayers of the saints, went up before God out of the angel's hand. And the angel took the censer; and he filled it with the fire of the altar and threw it to the earth; and there followed peals of thunder and sounds and flashes of lightning and an earthquake."

God answers the prayers of the saints in the trumpet and bowl judgments. Each judgment escalates the destruction of the earth, and torment and death to mankind.

"The seal judgments were rather general. The trumpet judgments are more specific. They are drastic but not universal."[319]

The first four trumpets describe what could be man-made disasters that are a likely result of nuclear warfare. The kind of destruction involved in the first two trumpets includes:

> First Trumpet Judgment: Hail, fire, blood, and the destruction of one third of earth, trees, and all grass.
> Second Trumpet Judgment: One third of seas become blood, one third of sea creatures die, one third of ships destroyed.

A nuclear blast would cause ice and fire to fall to the earth. The blood is self-explanatory. "The kind of destruction John describes is what today's 'think tanks' theorize will happen if all of these nations let a few of their favorite nukes fly at their favorite enemies."[320]

The third trumpet refers to a star falling from heaven like a torch on a third of the rivers and springs of waters. The star is called "Wormwood." Many people die because the waters are made bitter (Revelation 8:10-11).

Although it is not clear what the actual composition of "Wormwood" is, "from the preposition used in Greek, it is clear that it is of extraterrestrial origin."[321] This may be the result of a comet or meteor. Whatever the nature of the cause from a human standpoint, it is an awesome judgment of God resulting in the loss of many lives.

The fourth trumpet blocks out one third of the light from the sun, moon, and stars (Revelation 8:12). "Just as the first three trumpets dealt with a third of the earth, so the fourth trumpet dealt with a third of the heavens."[322]

Given the likelihood of a nuclear holocaust prior to this trumpet, it is reasonable to expect what scientists call the "nuclear winter" effect. There is so much debris kicked up into the atmosphere that day turns into night.[323]

There is no way to know exactly how the light from the sun, moon, and stars will be decreased by one third. We can see a similarity of some of these judgments to the plagues in Egypt. For example, the Lord caused darkness as one of the plagues over the Egyptians (Exodus 10:21-22).

The first four trumpets were primarily against nature (ecological damage). The last three are more severe and are directed against mankind.[324] "To this point, all the destruction, havoc and misery that we have witnessed has been essentially man-made. God ordained it in heaven, but he allowed it to take place through natural means."[325]

THE DEMONIC TRUMPETS: THE FINAL TRUMPETS

The fifth trumpet takes on a supernatural demonic nature against only the unbelievers. "And the fifth angel sounded, and I saw a star from heaven which had fallen to the earth; and the key to the bottomless pit was given to him. And he opened the bottomless pit . . ." (Revelation 9:1-2 NASB).

Walvoord and Zuck provide an interpretation of these two verses. In reference to the "he" in verse 2, and "king" in verse 11, they conclude that the star is probably a personality. The identity of the star probably represents Satan being cast out of heaven (Revelation 12:9). The "abyss" is considered the home of the demons (Luke 8:31; Rev. 9:11, 11:7, 17:8, 20:1,3; in Romans 10:7 it is translated as "deep").[326]

Out of the pit came creatures called locusts but which had a deadly sting like scorpions (Revelation 9:3, 5). These demonic creatures manifest themselves as locusts. We know these locusts are demonic beings because of verse 11. "And they have as king over them, the angel of the abyss; his name in Hebrew is Abaddon. . . ." "Abaddon" means destruction or destroyer.

These locusts are allowed to sting any person who does not have the seal of God on his forehead. They could torment but not kill anyone (Revelation 9:4-6). This seal of God on the foreheads of the true believers is God's protection. "This protection will extend to all believers (2 Timothy 2:19): The torment is a judgment on men who reject Christ. The protection also refers to the 144,000 who are already sealed (see Revelation 7). There is a sense in which all believers are sealed (Eph 1:13-14). But in that time there will be a seal in their foreheads."[327]

The unbelievers will seek death but cannot find it (Revelation 9:6). The unbeliever hardens his heart rather than turn to Christ.

The Antichrist Would Like to See Your I.D.

During the tribulation period, primarily the last three and one-half years, the Antichrist will require identification. This identification will allow the person to "buy or sell" (transact business) (Revelation 13:17).

Our world is moving electronically in a direction that would lay the groundwork for a massive identification process. "With the increasing move toward a cashlessness in our society, and with electronic banking already here, the addition of electronic shopping, world-wide connectivity, and global interdependence sure make the prophecy of the mark of the Beast seem a lot more realistic than it would even ten years ago."[328]

The mark of the beast is connected to allegiance with and worship of the Antichrist. By having the mark on the forehead or right hand, a person is identified as a worshiper of the Antichrist and, therefore, has the right to buy or sell (Revelation 13:15-17). The mark is the number 666.

Countless attempts have been made to identify what the number means. "Probably the best interpretation is that the number six is one less than the perfect number seven, and the threefold repetition of the six would indicate that for all their pretensions to deity, Satan and the two beasts were just creatures and not the Creator."[329]

Just as God sealed His 144,000 Jewish evangelists right after the sixth seal in Revelation 7:4, the Antichrist seals his followers. There are a number of people who are saved during the tribulation period and many will be martyred for their faith.

In this day and age (the Church Age), Christians can conceal their identity. In many cases it is difficult to discern who is a true believer in Jesus Christ. During the Great Tribulation, you are marked by God or by Satan (through the Antichrist). Your loyalty is established.

The leader of this worship system or one world religion is the False Prophet. According to Dwight Pentecost, the False Prophet is characterized by the following. "He promotes the worship of the first beast (the Antichrist). . . . He is successful in deceiving the unbelieving world (Revelation 13:14) . . . he has authority in the economic realm to control all commerce (13:16-17); he has a mark that will establish his identity for those who live in that day (13:18).[330]

We now have an establishment of an unholy or satanic trinity: the dragon, the beast, and the false prophet (Revelation 16:13). The place occupied by God the Father in this program is assumed by Satan (dragon), the place occupied by Christ is assumed by the first beast (Antichrist), and the ministry of the Holy Spirit is assumed by the False Prophet.[331]

Once the Antichrist has established his throne in the Jewish temple and established an identity system, he can now go after the Jews and the believers in Jesus Christ. "If he's learned anything from history, he's learned this equation: **Healthy Economy + Really Big Lie + Weak, but Plausible Excuse + Someone Else to Blame = Social Control**. It worked for Hitler. It seems to be working even better in the global arena."[332]

The Demonic Asian Invasion

The opening of the sixth trumpet has a flavor similar to the fifth trumpet. They both involve powerful demons or fallen angels. "And the sixth angel sounded, and I heard a voice from the four horns of the golden altar which is before God, one saying to the sixth angel who had the trumpet, 'Release the four angels who are bound at the great river Euphrates.' And the four angels, who had been prepared for the hour and day and month and year, were released, so that they might kill a third of mankind, and the number of the armies of the horsemen was two hundred million; I heard the number of them" (Revelation 9:13-16 NASB).

These four angels are demonic beings; this is demonstrated by the fact that they were "bound" at the river Euphrates. Good angels aren't bound. The demonic beings are then released to kill one third of mankind.

The river Euphrates was considered a natural boundary between the East and West. According to the Bible, demons are territorial and are assigned areas of authority. They are subject to Satan's authority over the world system. Human affairs are influenced by these territorial demons.[333]

These four demonic beings are the energizing force behind the 200 million man invasion. We know that this army comes from the East (probably China) and it crosses the river Euphrates on dry ground (Revelation 16:12).

When John wrote the Book of Revelation, a military force that numbered 200 million could not be imagined in the first century A.D. Today the Chinese army, which includes reserves, is well over 300 million.[334]

This massive invasion is also referred to in the sixth bowl judgment. Time-wise, we are moving rapidly toward Armageddon.

One third of mankind are killed during this invasion. The remainder of mankind who were not killed refuse to repent of their murders, sorceries, and immorality or thefts (Revelation 9:21). The combination of the occult coupled with drug use is the derivative for the translation of "sorceries." It is derived from the word "pharmakeion" which is translated "pharmacies."[335] Participation in the occult and the use of drugs will be at an all time high.

In the year 1999 A.D., the world population passed the 6 billion mark. The fourth seal kills one fourth of the world population. The sixth trumpet kills one third of the population. In other words, the world population is cut in half. In less than seven years, the world population would be reduced by 3 billion people, if the sixth trumpet judgment happened today. It is no wonder that Jesus said ". . . unless those days had been cut short, no life would have been saved; but for the sake of the elect those days shall be cut short" (Matthew 24:22 NASB).

THE FINAL STRETCH:
GOD'S WRATH ON EARTH - BOWL JUDGMENTS

These bowl judgments are the content of the seventh trumpet judgment. This trumpet judgment takes us to the end of the seven-year tribulation period. God's wrath concludes in the bowl judgments.[336]

These bowl judgments are very similar in nature to the plagues in Egypt. The difference is the intensity, plus the bowls are worldwide. Some of the bowls, like the plagues in Egypt, are inflicted only on the unbelievers.

First Bowl: Malignant Sores

"And the first angel went and poured out his bowl into the earth; and it became a loathsome and malignant sore upon the men who had the mark of the beast and who worshiped his image" (Revelation 16:2 NASB).

Only those who worship the Antichrist receive this cancerous sore; believers in Jesus are spared this judgment.

Second Bowl:
Sea Turns to Blood / All Sea Creatures Die

"And the second angel poured out his bowl into the sea, and it became blood like that of a dead man; and every living thing in the sea died" (Revelation 16:3 NASB).

It is horrifying to imagine every sea creature dead and floating to the surface. The stench and disease would be unbearable. **Planet earth is dying and it is not because there is a lack of environmental concern. There is a lack of God concern.** The rebellious, sinful nature of man is destroying our planet that was created by God.

Third Bowl:
Rivers and Springs Turn to Blood

"And the third angel poured out his bowl into the rivers and the springs of waters; and they became blood . . . for they poured out the blood of saints and prophets, and Thou hast given them blood to drink. They deserve it. And I heard those under the altar saying, 'Yes, O Lord God, the Almighty, true and righteous are Thy judgments'" (Revelation 16:4-7 NASB).

This is another judgment against the unbelievers. "The prayer of the martyred saints in Revelation 6:10 will be abundantly answered. They asked, 'How long, O Lord, holy and true, until You judge and avenge our blood on those who dwell on the earth?' This plague of blood is God's answer."[337] This is a judgment of vengeance on those who spilled the blood of the saints (believers in Jesus Christ).

Fourth Bowl:
Men Scorched With Heat

"The fourth angel poured out his bowl on the sun, and the sun was given power to scorch people with fire. They were seared by the intense heat and they cursed the name of God, who had control over these plagues, but they refused to repent and glorify him" (Revelation 16:8-9 NIV).

This judgment literally turns up the heat. Men are scorched and burned by the intense heat. The atmosphere that filters and protects us from the intense heat and ultraviolet rays is supernaturally removed.

This judgment is in contrast to the fourth trumpet where light diminishes by one third. God, our Creator, has total and absolute control over our climate and weather patterns.

In spite of the intense heat and men being scorched with fire, they do not repent. In their rebellion, they blaspheme the name of

God. They are not only seared by the heat, they also have a seared heart.

Fifth Bowl: Darkness

"And the fifth angel poured out his bowl upon the throne of the beast; and his kingdom became darkened; and they gnawed their tongues because of pain, and they blasphemed the God of heaven because of their pains and their sores; and they did not repent of their deeds" (Revelation 16:10-11 NASB).

This judgment is focused directly toward the Antichrist. This is a special judgment to show the world where the source of their trouble lies. When the Antichrist proclaims himself as God, he brings on God's wrath. God shows the world who the real God is.[338]

It must have astonished the apostle John when this revelation was disclosed to him. Mankind is suffering from sores, horrible burns from the sun, and no fresh water. They gnawed their tongues because of pain, but still blasphemed God and refused to repent.

Sixth Bowl:
Euphrates River Dries Up

"And the sixth angel poured out his bowl upon the great river, the Euphrates; and its water was dried up, that the way might be prepared for the kings of the east. And I saw coming out of the mouth of the dragon and out of the mouth of the beast and out of the mouth of the false prophet, three unclean spirits like frogs; for they are spirits of demons, performing signs, which go out to the kings of the whole world, to gather them together for the war of the great day of God, the Almighty . . . and they gathered them together to the place which in Hebrew is called Har–Magedon" (Revelation 16:12-16 NASB).

The first four bowl judgments are world-wide, but the remaining three are localized.[339] The sixth bowl judgment involves the drying up of the Euphrates River to prepare the way for the "kings of the east" or the Asian invasion of 200 million men.

God parted the Red Sea to provide the Israelites an escape from Egypt. In the sixth bowl, He dries up the Euphrates to provide a passage way for the final battle of Armageddon.

Revelation 9, Trumpet Judgment 6, saw the release of the four fallen angels (demons) who were bound at the Euphrates River. They mobilized the 200 million men from the east for the invasion of Israel. Phase two of this operation is found in Revelation 16, under Bowl Judgment 6, to prepare the way by drying up the Euphrates river.

Almost in the same breath, we see a release of demonic supernatural activity (verses 13-14). "For they are spirits of demons, performing signs, which go out to the kings of the whole world, to gather them together . . ." (Revelation 16:14 NASB).

In the time remaining in the Great Tribulation, sorcery is at an all time high. In reference to the world church (mystery Babylon), Revelation 18:23 says, ". . . all the nations were deceived by your sorcery." God reveals Satan's use of sorcery, drugs, and the occult. Hal Lindsey calls it "a world stoned out of its gourd."[340] This is the New Age movement at its zenith. It is not as subtle as it may appear today.

The demons in verse 14 go out to the "kings of the world" and "perform signs" to bring them together for the final battle. This is the battle at Armageddon.

Seventh Bowl: "It Is Done" -
Lightning, Thunder, Earthquake, Hail

"And the seventh angel poured out his bowl upon the air; and a loud voice came out of the temple from the throne, saying, 'It is done'" (Revelation 16:17 NASB).

This is followed by lightning, thunder, and a great earthquake (16:18). The magnitude of this earthquake is beyond imagination. "The city of Jerusalem will split into three parts. The cities of the nations fall (like London, Paris, Hong Kong) and Babylon the Great is destroyed (Rev 18). Every island fled away (Rev 6:14)."[341]

"And huge hailstones, about one hundred pounds each, came down from heaven upon men; and men blasphemed God because of the plague of the hail, because its plague was extremely severe" (Revelation 16:21 NASB).

The Lord will literally stone people to death. The law required that a blasphemer be stoned to death (Leviticus 24:16). God will enforce the law in a very big way.

ANTICHRIST AND FALSE PROPHET: AN ALIEN CONNECTION?

Earlier in this chapter, we discussed the possibility of the Antichrist having some type of alien connection. Remember the world is moving toward the New Age belief in monism which is a disregard of a dualistic system. It is an "all is one" belief system.

Add ET's and UFO's to a monistic belief system to produce a world view that is fertile for a demonic deception in the latter times. Once the Rapture has occurred, belief in ET's and UFO's will mushroom.

It is very likely that demonic activity will be disguised through the belief in aliens. There is a growing belief that aliens are our creators.

The scientific community led by NASA and various scientific academies are continually looking for confirmation of life on other planets. Millions of people look to the skies for our space brothers to save us from our advancing planetary predicament.[342]

There is a "prevailing view that our highly evolved ancestors with incredibly advanced technology have prepared the world to receive them as our technological saviors . . . the stage is set for the worship and reverence of alien entities. . . ."[343]

ARMAGEDDON: THE FINAL CONFLICT

The final battle of Armageddon is the result of a world war. This war is a result of demon spirits that draw the kings of the whole world together for war (Revelation 16:14).

The Bible describes four destructive spheres of power in the last days. We have the northern powers (which include Russia); the kings of the East (the Asian power); the revived Roman Empire (led by the Antichrist); and the Kings of the South (Pan-Arab power).[344]

This final battle will produce a blood bath that cannot be rivaled. Revelation 14:20 states, ". . . the wine press was trodden outside the city, and blood came out from the wine press, up to the horses' bridles, for a distance of two hundred miles."

"Armageddon" is a translation from the Greek "Harmagedon" which is the transliteration of the Hebrew words for Mount (bar) of Megiddo. "That mountain is near the city of Megiddo and the plain of Esdraelon, the scene of many Old Testament battles."[345]

The final battle of Armageddon in Revelation 16 is from God's point of view. In Revelation 19, we see the final battle from man's point of view.[346]

HEAVEN'S INVASION

And I saw heaven opened; and behold, a white horse, and He who sat upon it is called Faithful and True; and in righteousness He judges and wages war. And His eyes are a flame of fire, and upon His head are many diadems; and He has a name written upon Him which no one knows except Himself. And He is clothed with a robe dipped in blood; and His name is called The Word of God. And the armies which are in heaven, clothed in fine linen, white and clean, were following Him on white horses. And from His mouth comes a sharp sword, so that with it He may smite the nations;

> and He will rule them with a rod of iron; and He treads the wine press of the fierce wrath of God, the Almighty. And on His robe and on His thigh He has a name written, "KING OF KINGS, AND LORD OF LORDS" (Revelation 19:11-16 NASB).

Jesus came the first time 2000 years ago and died a cruel death on a wooden cross. He shed His blood to pay the ultimate sacrifice for man's sins. The first time He came as a lamb with a love beyond our understanding. He returns as the Lion of Judah.

When Jesus Christ returns, He cuts through all the dimensions of space and time. The infinite Lord of the universe, Jesus of Nazareth, comes back in glory. It will be beautiful to those that have turned to Him and terrifying to those who have hardened their hearts.

C. S. Lewis describes the Second Coming in his book, *Mere Christianity*, as follows:

> God is going to invade, all right: but what is the good of saying you are on His side then, when you see the whole natural universe melting away like a dream and something else – something it never entered your head to conceive – comes crashing in; something so beautiful to some of us and so terrible to others that none of us will have any choice left? For this time it will be God without disguise; something so overwhelming that it will strike either irresistible love or irresistible horror into every creature. It will be too late then to choose your side. There is no use saying you choose to lie down when it has become impossible to stand up. That will not be the time for choosing: it will be the time when we discover which side we really have chosen, whether we realized it or not. Now, today, this moment, is our chance to choose the right side. God is holding back to give us that chance. It will not last for ever. We must take it or leave it.

THE FINAL ACT

"It is a terrifying thing to fall into the hands of the living God" (Hebrews 10:31 NASB). This will be the fate of everyone who rejects Jesus Christ.

The following poem, by an anonymous author, is quoted by Chuck Swindoll in *The Grace Awakening* and in *The Tail of the Tardy Ox Cart*:

> If our greatest need had been information, God would have sent us an educator.
> If our greatest need had been technology, God would have sent us a scientist.
> If our greatest need had been money, God would have sent us an economist.
> If our greatest need had been pleasure, God would have sent us a treasure.
> But our greatest need was forgiveness, so God sent us a Savior!

C. S. Lewis, a professor at Cambridge University and once an agnostic, discussed man's options concerning Jesus' identity. To accept Jesus as a great moral teacher, but not accept His claim to be God, is really foolish, according to Lewis. For Jesus to be a mere man and to make the statements He made, He would have to be a "lunatic" or the "devil of Hell." Jesus either "was and is, the Son of God, or else a madman or something worse."[347]

The argument C.S. Lewis proposes concerning Jesus is that we have three choices:
1. Jesus was a liar.
2. Jesus was a lunatic.
3. Jesus is Lord.

There are no other alternatives. Jesus stands at the door of your heart and knocks (Revelation 3:20). His gift of salvation is free (Ephesians 2:8-9). If you would like to ask Jesus into your heart, pray the following suggested prayer (or you can use your own words):

> *Lord Jesus, I need you. Thank you for dying on the cross for my sins. I open the door to my life and receive You as my Savior and Lord. Thank you for forgiving my sins. Make me the kind of person you want me to be.*

If you prayed this prayer and it was the desire of your heart, you are saved. He promised it. You are a child of God (John 1:12).

If you ask Jesus into your life prior to the Rapture, I'll meet you at the Rapture. If you pray this after the Rapture, I'll meet you at the Second Coming.

"... And lo, I am with you always, even to the end of the age" (Matthew 28:20 NASB).

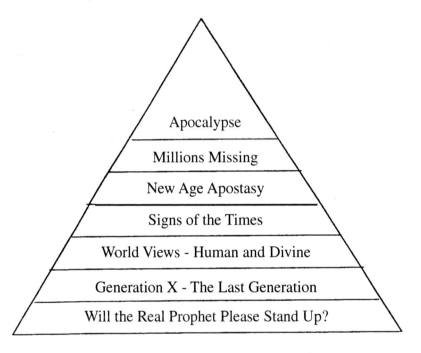

APPENDIX A

For The Reader's Consideration

This book was written to answer some very critical questions about life, truth, meaning, and one's source of authority. One of the primary purposes of this book was to guide the reader in answering the following questions:
1. What is truth?
2. Where do I find it?
3. How do I know that my source of truth is reliable?
4. When I know the truth, what does it mean to me?
5. What are my choices once I know the truth?
6. What are the outcomes of my choices?

When answering the above questions, the reader may want to consider the following "what if" questions:
1. What if - the Bible was shown to be the Word of God and contains ultimate truth?
2. What if - the Bible says that Jesus is the Way, the Truth, and the Life, and no one comes to God but through Him?
3. What if - the Bible says that man is a sinner and cannot be saved by his own good works?
4. What if - the Bible says that Jesus paid the penalty for my sins by dying on the cross?
5. What if - the Bible said I could be saved from eternal judment by taking the following steps?
   A. Believe Jesus died for my sins and was resurrected (John 3:16; I Cor.15:14).
   B. Ask Him in prayer to come into my life (Rev.3:20).

WOULD I DO IT?

The following are a few of the points covered in this book. Points 1 - 5 cover the foundation for our Biblical source of authority. Points 6 - 14 cover a few of the reasons to believe that the Rapture is right at the door.

1. The Bible is God's Word as established by historical prophecy fulfillment (see Chapter One).
2. Jesus fulfills 333 Old Testament prophecies as the Messiah (see Chapter One).
3. The miraculous rebirth of the nation Israel in 1948. It had not been a sovereign nation for over 2500 years, but the Old Testament prophesied it in Ezekiel 37:11-14 (see Chapter Two).
4. The literal prophetic fulfillment of the 70 weeks of Daniel 9:24-27 (see Chart One).
5. Jesus prophesied the destruction of Jerusalem because they rejected Him as their Messiah (Luke 19:41-44). This was fulfilled when the Romans under Titus overthrew Jerusalem in 70 A.D.
6. The exponential increase in the signs preceding the Second Coming of Christ, as shown in the increase in earthquakes (refer to Chart 3) and the exponential increase in knowledge (refer to Chart 6).
7. The prediction of the nearness of the end times from the secular (non-biblical) scientist's viewpoint.
8. Evidence of the movement toward a one world government (see Chapter Four) which will characterize the tribulation period (Revelation 13).
9. The parable of the fig tree. Within one generation of the establishment of Israel as a nation (1948), Jesus will return at the Second Coming (see Chapter Two).
10. A counterfeit rapture proposed by the New Age authors to deceive the people who are left behind when the Biblical Rapture happens (see Chapters Five and Six).
11. How high tech communication networks have laid the groundwork for a one world government and banking system (see Chapter Four).
12. The movement toward rebuilding the Jewish temple (see Chapter Seven).

13. The chance of Jesus fulfilling only fifty out of the 333 Old Testament prophecies are one in 1,125,000,000,000,000, according to the theory of probabilities (see Chapter One).
14. Certain events must take place in the last generation, including the rebirth of Israel as a nation, revival of the old Roman Empire (modern Europe), and the formation of a worldwide government through peace. These events have already happened or are in the process of happening. This would make our generation the last generation (see Chapter Five).

Appendix B

LIST OF TRIBULATION JUDGMENTS
(SEALS, TRUMPETS, AND BOWLS)

SEAL JUDGMENTS (7)

1. White horse - conqueror (Rev. 6:1-2)
   (Antichrist in power; first half of tribulation period - 3 1/2 years peace)

2. Red horse - war (Rev. 6:3-4)
   (Antichrist begins second half of tribulation period - "The Great Tribulation")

3. Black horse - famine (Rev. 6:5-6)
   (starvation/poverty)

4. Pale Horse - Death and Hades (Rev. 6:7-8)
   (kills one-fourth of the population - by weapons, starvation & disease)

5. Saints martyred cry out under altar in heaven (Rev. 6:9-11)
   (Antichrist killing believers)

6. Great earthquake, sun - black, moon - red, sky - split; stars fall (Rev. 6:12-17)
   (every mountain and island moved. People say to the mountains "fall on us," hide us from the wrath of the Lamb, the anger of God)

7. Silence in heaven - 30 minutes; earthquake, thunder, lightning; this opens the trumpet judgments (Rev. 8:1-5)

TRUMPET JUDGMENTS (7)

1. Hail - fire - blood - destroy 1/3 of the earth, 1/3 of the trees & all grass (Rev. 8:7)

2. Seas struck - 1/3 becomes blood; 1/3 of sea creatures die; 1/3 of ships destroyed; like mountain of fire thrown into sea (Rev. 8:8-9)

3. Wormwood (star) falls on 1/3 of the rivers and springs; many die from bitter waters (Rev. 8:10-11)

4. Heavens struck; 1/3 of the sun, moon and stars do not shine (Rev. 8:12)

5. Locusts from the Bottomless Pit. Five months of torment for unbelievers (Rev. 9:1-11)

6. Four angels released - 200 million horsemen - kill 1/3 of people with fire, smoke, and brimstone; mighty angel with a little book (Rev. 9:13-21)

7. Kingdom of God and Jesus Christ proclaimed. Lightning, thunder, earthquake, and hail announce the approaching end (Rev. 11:15-19)

BOWL JUDGMENTS (7)

1. Malignant sores on those with mark of the beast and who worship the image of the beast (Rev. 16:2)

2. All the sea turns to blood; all sea creatures die (Rev. 16:3)

3. All rivers and springs turn to blood (Rev. 16:4-7)

4. Men scorched with fire and heat (Rev. 16:8-9)

5. Darkness and pain (Rev. 16:10-11)

6. Euphrates River dries up. Demon spirits gather kings of world to battle (Rev. 16:12)

7. Final bowl. Thunder, lightning, great earthquake; islands disappear, mountains flatten; hail of 100 pounds (Rev. 16:17-21)

Then Christ returns on a white horse with the armies of heaven (Rev. 19:11-16). Satan is bound for 1,000 years. Saints from the Tribulation reign with Christ for 1,000 years (Rev. 20:4).

At the end of the 1,000 years, Satan is released (Rev. 20:7). The final battle occurs (Rev. 20:8-9). The devil is cast into the lake of fire where the beast and the false prophet are and will be tormented day and night forever (Rev. 20:10).

Great White Throne Judgment - unbelievers judged (Rev. 20:11-12).

New Heaven and a New Earth: New Jerusalem comes down out of heaven. No more death, sorrow, crying (Rev. 21:1-4).

"I am the Alpha and the Omega, the first and the last, the beginning and the end" (Rev. 21:13).

Come soon, Lord Jesus!

FOOTNOTES

1. *Dallas Morning News*, October 15, 1999, Morning Briefcase, Forward Thinking, p. 2D.
2. IBID.
3. Christine Simmons, *Prophecy*, Southwestern Typographics, 1976, p. 1-2.
4. Josh McDowell, *Evidence That Demands a Verdict*, Here's Life Publishers, 1972, Campus Crusade for Christ, p. 16.
5. *Denton Record Chronicle*, December 3, 1999, Scientists Eye Noah's Flood, Religion, p. 1B.
6. McDowell, *Evidence That Demands a Verdict*, p. 22.
7. Hal Lindsey, *Apocalypse Code*, Western Front Ltd., 1997, p. 48.
8. IBID., p. 64.
9. McDowell, *Evidence That Demands a Verdict*, p. 269.
10. Chuck Missler and Mark Eastman, *Alien Encounters*, Koinonia House, 1997, p. 225.
11. McDowell, *Evidence That Demands a Verdict*, p. 274-302. These pages give all of the specific historical fulfillments and details that surround each prophecy.
12. IBID., p. 320.
13. Lindsey, *Apocalypse Code*, p. 55.
14. IBID., p. 57.
15. IBID., p. 60.
16. IBID., p. 61.
17. IBID., p. 61.
18. Simmons, p. 8.
19. McDowell, *Evidence That Demands a Verdict*, p. 170.
20. IBID., p. 170.
21. Simmons, p. 8-9.
22. Hal Lindsey, *Planet Earth: The Final Chapter*, Western Front Ltd., 1998, p. 78.
23. Missler and Eastman, p. 227-228.
24. Daniel 9:24 (NASB).
25. J. Dwight Pentecost, *Things To Come*, Zondervan, 1974, p. 241.
26. McDowell, *Evidence That Demands a Verdict*, p. 172.
27. Pentecost, *Things to Come*, p. 244.
28. IBID., p. 244.

29. McDowell, *Evidence That Demands a Verdict*, p. 173.
30. IBID., p. 173 (Quote within from Harold Hoehner, *Chronological Aspects of the Life of Christ*, Zondervan, 1977, p. 138).
31. For other charts of Daniel's 70 weeks, see: McDowell, *Evidence That Demands a Verdict*, p. 174; Walvoord and Zuck, *The Bible Knowledge Commentary, Old Testament*, p. 1363; and Missler and Eastman, p. 232.
32. Missler and Eastman, p. 234.
33. John Walvoord, *Major Bible Prophecies*, Zondervan, 1991, p. 207.
34. Fred John Meldau, *Messiah in Both Testaments*, Christian Victory Publishing, 1956, p. 5.
35. IBID., p. 5.
36. IBID., p. 8.
37. McDowell, *Evidence That Demands a Verdict*, p. 315.
38. Pentecost, p. 317.
39. Lindsay, *Planet Earth: The Final Chapter*, Western Front Ltd., 1998, p. 81.
40. IBID., p. 82.
41. Simmons, p. 15.
42. Missler and Eastman, p. 274.
43. For developments in Europe, see briefing package, *Iron Mixed with Clay*, Koinonia House, Missler and Eastman.
44. Simmons, p. 14.
45. Lindsay, *Planet Earth: The Final Chapter*, p. 69.
46. IBID., p. 96.
47. IBID., p. 97. (These nine points are found in Matthew 24:4-7; Luke 21: 25, 26).
48. Matthew 24:4-7; Luke 21:8-26; Mark 13:6-25; Daniel 12:4; II Thessalonians 2:3; I Timothy 4:1-3; Revelation 9:21; and II Timothy 4:3.
49. Missler and Eastman, p. 182.
50. IBID., p. 183.
51. IBID., p. 170.
52. Lindsey, *Apocalypse Code*, p. 296.
53. Missler and Eastman, p. 171.

54. *Denton Record Chronicle*, Wednesday, November 3, 1999, World Briefs, p. 8A (as quoted from Klaus Toepfer, head of the U.N. Environment Program).
55. Lindsey, *Apocalypse Code*, p. 296.
56. IBID., p. 14.
57. IBID., p. 13.
58. Missler and Eastman, p. 165.
59. *Denton Record Chronicle*, Wednesday, November 3, 1999, World Briefs, p. 8A.
60. Missler and Eastman, p. 172.
61. Lindsey, *Planet Earth: The Final Chapter,* p. 105.
62. IBID., p. 105.
63. IBID., p. 105-106.
64. Missler and Eastman, p. 173.
65. Billy Graham, *Approaching Hoofbeats: The Four Horsemen of the Apocalypse*, Word Books, Inc., 1983, p. 135.
66. Lindsey, *Apocalypse Code*, p. 177.
67. IBID., p. 295.
68. Chip Ingram, "What We Must Learn From the Killings at Columbine High," Living on the Edge, P.O. Box 2370, Santa Cruz, California (Sermon), 1999.
69. IBID.
70. Lindsey, *Apocalypse Code*, p. 178.
71. International Christian Concern, "Global Persecution Update: Pakistan," August 9, 1998 (www. Presecution.org).
72. International Christian Concern, "Top–Ten Priority Watch List of Countries Where Christians Are Persecuted," October 22, 1998 (www.Persecution.org).
73. Nina Shea, *In the Lion's Den: A Shocking Account of the Persecution and Martyrdom of Christians Today and How We Should Respond*, Broadman and Holman, 1997, p. 1.
74. *Lindsey, Apocalypse Code,* p. 299.
75. IBID., p. 137.
76. IBID., p. 137.
77. Peter and Paul Lalonde, *2000 A.D.*, Thomas Nelson, 1997, p. 34.
78. Lindsey, *Apocalypse Code,* p. 10 (Quotation from Dr. George Wald, Nobel prize-winning scientist, Harvard University).

79. Hal Lindsey, *Satan Is Alive and Well on Plant Earth*, Zondervan, 1972, p. 85.
80. IBID., p. 86.
81. Francis Schaeffer, *The God Who Is There*, InterVarsity Press, 1968, by L'Abri Fellowship, p. 20.
82. Lindsey, *Satan Is Alive and Well on Planet Earth*, p. 86.
83. Schaeffer, p. 21.
84. Lindsey, *Satan Is Alive and Well on Planet Earth*, p. 91.
85. Desmond Morris, *The Naked Ape,* McGraw-Hill, 1969.
86. Lindsey, *Satan Is Alive and Well on Planet Earth*, p. 92.
87. Schaeffer, p. 93.
88. Dr. A. A. Brill, *The Basic Writings of Sigmund Freud*, Random House, 1938.
89. Boris Sokoloff, *The Permissive Society,* Arlington House, 1971.
90. Joel Kovel, *A Complete Guide To Therapy: From Psychoanalysis to Behavioral Modification*, Pantheon Books, 1976, p. 93.
91. IBID., p. 100.
92. IBID., p. 92.
93. IBID., p. 109.
94. IBID., p. 113.
95. IBID., p. 149.
96. Lindsey, *Satan Is Alive and Well on Planet Earth*, p. 100.
97. *Time*, September 30, 1971.
98. Kovel, p. 42.
99. Howard Becker, *Outsiders,* The Free Press, 1963, p. 5.
100. Martin L. Gross, *The Psychological Society,* Random House, 1978, p. 16.
101. Frank Minirth and Paul Meier, *Counseling and the Nature of Man*, Baker Book House, 1982, p. 10.
102. Viktor E. Frankl, *Man's Search for Meaning*, Pocket Books, Simon and Schuster, 1963, p. 154.
103. Minirth and Meier, p. 13.
104. IBID., p. 7.
105. Viktor E. Frankl, p. 153.
106. Lindsey, *Satan is Alive and Well on Planet Earth*, p. 53.
107. Neil T. Anderson, *The Bondage Breaker*, Harvest House Publishers, 1990, p. 53.

108. IBID., p. 83.
109. IBID., p. 99.
110. Minirth and Meier, p. 10-11.
111. Missler and Eastman, p. 149.
112. Schaeffer, p. 17.
113. Proverbs 14:12 NASB.
114. Minirth and Meier, p. 10.
115. Missler and Eastman, p. 153.
116. Schaeffer, p. 62.
117. IBID., p. 61.
118. Alcoholics Anonymous, Alcoholics Anonymous World Services, 1976, p. 53.
119. Lalonde, p. 9.
120. IBID., p. 23.
121. IBID., p. 21-22.
122. IBID., p. 4.
123. IBID., p. 165.
124. IBID., p. 168.
125. *Time* Magazine, Dec. 6, 1999, p. 1 (Agilent Technologies Innovating the HP Way).
126. Lalonde, p. 174.
127. Missler and Eastman, p. 162.
128. Art Bell, *The Art of Talk*, Paper Chase Press, 1995, p. 141-142.
129. Missler and Eastman, p. 183.
130. Lalonde, p. 88 (Parenthesis by author).
131. IBID., p. 89.
132. IBID., p. 82.
133. IBID., p. 99.
134. IBID., p. 141.
135. IBID., p. 116.
136. IBID., p. 138.
137. IBID., p. 140.
138. IBID., p. 134-135.
139. *Dallas Morning News*, Thursday Jan. 4, 2000, "CBS's Digital Imaging Raises Ethical Storm," p. 4A.
140. Lalonde, p. 146.
141. IBID., p. 123.

142. IBID., p. 123.
143. IBID., p. 15.
144. IBID., p. 126.
145. Lindsey, *Apocalypse Code,* p. 186.
146. IBID., p. 103.
147. Tim LaHaye and Jerry Jenkins, *Are We Living In the End Times?* Tyndale House Publishers, 1999, p. 169.
148. Lindsey, *Apocalypse Code,* p. 103.
149. IBID., p. 104.
150. IBID., p. 210.
151. IBID., p. 298.
152. IBID., p. 297.
153. *Dallas Morning News,* October 15, 1999, "White House, Fed Strikes Deal on Banks," p. 2D.
154. Terry L. Cook, *The Mark of the New World Order,* Whitaker House, 1996, p. 204.
155. *Denton Record Chronicle*, November 15, 1999, p. 1A.
156. Lindsey, *Planet Earth: The Final Chapter,* p. 92.
157. IBID., p. 90.
158. Lindsey, *Apocalypse Code,* p. 107.
159. Missler and Eastman, p. 145.
160. Lalonde, p. 44.
161. Lindsey, *Apocalypse Code,* p. 209.
162. IBID., p. 209.
163. Anderson, p. 32.
164. *UFO Universe* (September 1998), p. 32.
165. Anderson, p. 122.
166. Missler and Eastman, p. 149.
167. IBID., p. 323.
168. *Denton Record Chronicle*, Friday October 22, 1999, "Denton Unitarian Church Lands 50 Year Milestone," p. 1B.
169. James Redfield, *The Celestine Prophecy*, Warner Books, 1993, p. 24.
170. Barbara Hubbard, *The Revelation*, Nataraj Publishing, 1995, p. 192.
171. IBID., p. 15.
172. IBID., p. 187.
173. Redfield, p. 239.

174. Lalonde, p. 53.
175. Anderson, p. 80.
176. Lindsey, *Planet Earth: The Final Chapter*, p 137-138 (quoted in part from 2102 Unlimited, New Age Internet Group, June 2, 1998).
177. William M. Alnor, *UFO's in the New Age*, Baker Book House, 1992, p. 53-54.
178. Hubbard, p. 271.
179. Redfield, p. 241.
180. Lindsey, *Planet Earth: The Final Chapter*, p. 82.
181. Lindsey, *Apocalypse Code,* p. 205.
182. Lindsey, *Planet Earth: The Final Chapter*, p. 145.
183. Lalonde, p. 156.
184. *Denton Record Chronicle*, Oct. 22, 1999, "Denton Unitarian Church Lands 50 Year Milestone," p. 1B.
185. IBID.
186. Missler and Eastman, p. 150.
187. IBID., p. 178.
188. Lindsey, *Planet Earth: The Final Chapter*, p. 90.
189. Lindsey, *Apocalypse Code,* p. 174.
190. Lalonde, p. 154.
191. Missler and Eastman, p. 302.
192. IBID., p. 145.
193. Lindsey, *Planet Earth: The Final Chapter*, p. 91-92.
194. William M. Alnor, *UFO's in the New Age*, Baker Book House, 1993, p. 73 (quoting Douglas Curran, *In Advance of Landing: Folk Concepts of Outer Space,* New York: Aberville Press, 1985, p. 4).
195. Missler and Eastman, p. 9 (as quoted from Gallup polls done in 1991 and 1996).
196. Missler and Eastman, p. 9 (as quoted from George M. Eberhart, *UFOs and the Extraterrestrial Contact Movement: A Bibliography*, 2 Vol., Scarecrow Press, London, 1986.
197. Missler and Eastman, p. 12 (sources include: Brit Elders, Connecting Link Magazine, Issue 27, Spring 1995, p. 92; La Presna, Jan. 2, 1992; and Voyagers of the Sixth Sun, produced by Genesis III).
198. Missler and Eastman, p. 14.
199. Missler and Eastman, p. 15 (as quoted from *UFO Reality* February/March, 1997, Issue 6, p. 10).

200. Missler and Eastman, p. 15 (as quoted from UFO Reality February/March, 1997, Issue 6, p. 11).
201. *The Plain Dealer Newspaper,* March 31, 1996, Plain Dealer Publishing Co., p. 1F.
202. Timothy Good, *Above Top Secret,* William Marrow Co., 1988, p. 384.
203. Missler and Eastman, p. 28.
204. IBID., p. 28.
205. IBID., p. 55-56.
206. IBID., p. 56. As obtained from Lawrence Fawcett and Barry J. Greenwood, *Clear Intent: The Government Coverup of the UFO Experience,* Prentice-Hall, 1984.
207. Missler and Eastman, p. 57.
208. IBID., p. 66.
209. IBID., p. 32.
210. *Nature*, Nov. 12, 1981; 294:105.
211. Missler and Eastman, p. 129.
212. IBID., p. 134.
213. IBID., p. 67.
214. Tara Gravel, "Interview with David Jacobs, Ph.D.," Temple University Journalism Paper, December 6, 1990.
215. Alnor, p. 15.
216. Lalonde, p. 75.
217. Missler and Eastman, p. 35.
218. IBID., p. 38.
219. See Graham Hancock, *The Fingerprints of the Gods,* Crown Trade Paperbacks, 1995, and Graham Hancock and Robert Bauval, *The Message of the Sphinx*, Crown Publishers, 1996.
220. Missler and Eastman, p. 49.
221. IBID., p. 37.
222. IBID., p. 50.
223. I.D.E. Thomas, *The Omega Conspiracy,* Hearthstone Publishing, 1986, p. 84.
224. Missler and Eastman, p. 98.
225. IBID., p. 106-107.
226. IBID., p. 52.
227. IBID., p. 67.

228. Jacques Vallee, *Dimensions,* Ballantine Books, 1988, p. 252-253.
229. Missler and Eastman, p. 95.
230. IBID., p. 119-120.
231. Paul Davies, *God and the New Physics,* Simon and Schuster, 1983, p. 119.
232. Alnor, p. 237 (as quoted from Mark Albrecht and Brooks Alexander, "UFO's: Is Science Fiction Coming True?" *SCP Journal* 1, 1977, p. 21-22).
233. Missler and Eastman, p. 86 (as quoted from Edwin A. Abbott, 1836-1926, a distinguished clergyman, who wrote *Flatland* in 1884, an allegorical approach to dimensionality).
234. Missler and Eastman, p. 86.
235. IBID., p. 80.
236. Davies, p. 102.
237. IBID., p. 101.
238. IBID., p. 100.
239. IBID., p. 133-134.
240. IBID., p. 210.
241. Hugh Ross, Ph.D., *Beyond the Cosmos*, Nav Press, 1999, p. 51.
242. IBID., p. 51.
243. IBID., p. 52.
244. Alnor, p. 53-54.
245. IBID., p. 14.
246. IBID., p. 15.
247. Missler and Eastman, p. 187.
248. Alnor, p. 42-43 (as quoted from Stuart Goldman, unpublished manuscript on Whitley Strieber on file, cited in Alnor, "UFO Cults . . .").
249. Lalonde, p. 67.
250. Bible references declaring the occult wrong: Deuteronomy 18:10-11; Isaiah 47:9-13; Leviticus 19:31; Isaiah 8:19; and II Corinthians 11:14-15. These references include: witchcraft, astrology, mediums – channeling, and white magic. Also, the Book of Hosea is about Israel's spiritual adultery through idolatry.
251 Lindsay, *Planet Earth: The Final Chapter,* p. 125.
252. Lalonde, p. 54.
253. Redfield, p. 242.
254. Hubbard, p. 271.

255. Alnor, p. 55.
256. Ruth Montgomery, *Ruth Montgomery: Herald of the New Age*, Doubleday, 1986, p. 269.
257. Frank E. Stranges, *Stranger at the Pentagon*, Inner Light Publications, 1991, p. 125.
258. Missler and Eastman, p. 187.
259. Missler and Eastman, p. 189 (quoting Kay Wheeler, "The Time Is Now," *Connecting Link,* 23:34).
260. Hubbard, p. 197.
261. Missler and Eastman, p. 256.
262. IBID., p. 199.
263. John F. Walvoord and Roy B. Zuck, *The Bible Knowledge Commentary, Old Testament*, SP Publications, 1985, p. 127.
264. Simmons, p. 16.
265. John F. Walvoord, *Major Bible Prophecies*, Zondervan, 1991, p. 314.
266. IBID., p. 313.
267. IBID., p. 314.
268. Missler and Eastman, p. 234.
269. Pentecost, p. 137.
270. Tim LaHaye and Jerry Jenkins, *Are We Living In The End Times?* Tyndale House, 1999, p. 116.
271. Lindsey, *Planet Earth: The Final Chapter*, p. 150.
272. IBID., p. 77.
273. Lindsey, *Apocalypse Code*, p. 137.
274. Lindsey, *Planet Earth: The Final Chapter*, p. 200 (as quoted from Lindsey, *Apocalypse Code,* 1997).
275. Lindsey, *Apocalypse Code*, p. 154.
276. Pentecost, p. 215.
277. Lindsey, *Planet Earth: The Final Chapter*, p. 155.
278. LaHaye and Jenkins, p. 275-276.
279. Lindsey, *Planet Earth: The Final Chapter*, p. 158.
280. Missler and Eastman, p. 285.
281. IBID., p. 286.
282. Lalonde, p. 102-103.
283. John Walvoord, *The Revelation of Jesus Christ*, Moody Press, 1966, p. 178.

284. LaHaye and Jenkins, p. 304.
285. IBID., p. 311.
286. Lindsey, *Planet Earth: The Final Chapter*, p. 159.
287. IBID., p. 101.
288. John F. Walvoord and Roy B. Zuck, *The Bible Knowledge Commentary, New Testament*, SP Publications, 1983, p. 947.
289. Lindsey, *Planet Earth: The Final Chapter*, p. 172.
290. IBID. (as quoted from Daniel 8:25, literal translation from the Hebrew Masoretic text).
291. Walvoord, *Major Bible Prophecies*, p. 351.
292. Lindsey, *Planet Earth: The Final Chapter*, p. 160.
293. LaHaye and Jenkins, p. 122.
294. Thomas Ice and Timothy Demy, *The Truth About the Last Days' Temple*, Harvest House, 1997, p. 29.
295. Walvoord and Zuck, *The Bible Knowledge Commentary, New Testament*, p. 959.
296. Missler and Eastman, p. 321.
297. Alnor, p. 34.
298. IBID., p. 205.
299. John Mack, *Abduction*, Ballantine Books, 1994, p. 411.
300. Missler and Eastman, p. 259.
301. IBID., p. 259.
302. IBID., p. 260.
303. IBID., p. 261.
304. IBID., p. 275.
305. IBID., p. 276.
306. Walvoord and Zuck, *The Bible Knowledge Commentary, New Testament*, p. 948.
307. Walvoord, *Major Bible Prophecies*, p. 329-330.
308. Lindsey, *Planet Earth: The Final Chapter*, p. 182.
309. Simmons, p. 161-162.
310. Lindsey, *Planet Earth: The Final Chapter*, p. 180.
311. *Dallas Morning News*, January 1, 2000, p. 1A.
312. IBID., p. 29A.
313. Lindsey, *Planet Earth: The Final Chapter*, p. 213.
314. IBID., p. 227.
315. Simmons, p. 94-95.

316. IBID., p. 95.
317. Pentecost, *Things to Come*, p. 360.
318. Lindsey, *Planet Earth: The Final Chapter*, p. 200.
319. Simmons, p. 104.
320. Lindsey, *Planet Earth: The Final Chapter*, p. 208.
321. IBID., p. 226.
322. Walvoord and Zuck, *The Bible Knowledge Commentary, New Testament*, p. 952.
323. Lindsey, *Planet Earth: The Final Chapter*, p. 234.
324. Simmons, p. 110.
325. Lindsey, *Planet Earth: The Final Chapter*, p. 240.
326. Walvoord and Zuck, *The Bible Knowledge Commentary, New Testament*, p. 953.
327. Simmons, p. 113.
328. Lalonde, p. 174.
329. Walvoord and Zuck, *The Bible Knowledge Commentary, New Testament*, p. 963.
330. Pentecost, *Things To Come*, p. 337.
331. IBID., p. 337.
332. Lindsey, *Planet Earth: The Final Chapter*, p. 220.
333. IBID., p. 244.
334. IBID., p. 246.
335. Walvoord and Zuck, *The Bible Knowledge Commentary, New Testament*, p. 953.
336. Simmons, p. 144.
337. LaHaye and Jenkins, p. 207-208.
338. IBID., p. 208-209.
339. Simmons, p. 149.
340. Lindsey, *Planet Earth: The Final Chapter*, p. 261.
341. Simmons, p. 153.
342. Missler and Eastman, p. 261.
343. IBID., p. 261.
344. Lindsey, *Planet Earth: The Final Chapter*, p. 279.
345. Walvoord and Zuck, *The Bible Knowledge Commentary, New Testament*, p. 968.
346. Simmons, p. 152.
347. C. S. Lewis, *Mere Christianity*, Macmillan, 1947, p. 40-41.

BIBLIOGRAPHY

Alcoholics Anonymous. *"The Big Book."* New York: Alcoholics Anonymous World Services Inc., 1976.

Alnor, William M. *UFO's in the New Age.* Grand Rapids, MI: Baker Book House, 1992.

Anderson, Neil T. *The Bondage Breaker.* Eugene, OR: Harvest House Publishers, 1993.

Becker, Howard S. *Outsiders.* New York: The Free Press, 1973.

Bell, Art. *The Art of Talk.* New Orleans, LA: Paper Chase Press, 1995.

Brill, Dr. A. A. *The Basic Writings of Sigmund Freud.* New York, NY: Random House, 1938.

Cook, Terry L. *The Mark of the New World Order.* Springdale, PA: Whitaker House, 1996.

Dallas Morning News. October 15, 1999, Forward Thinking, 2D.

Dallas Morning News. January 1, 2000, 1A.

Dallas Morning News. January 4, 2000, "CBS's Digital Imaging Raises Ethical Storm," 4A.

Dallas Morning News. October 15, 1999, "White House, Fed Strikes Deal on Bombs," 2D.

Davies, Paul. *God and the New Physics.* New York, NY: Simon & Schuster, 1983.

Denton Record Chronicle. October 22, 1999, "Denton Unitarian Church Lands 50 Year Milestone," 1B.

Denton Record Chronicle. November 3, 1999, World Briefs, 8A.

Denton Record Chronicle. November 15, 1999, 1A.

Frankl, Viktor E. *Man's Search for Meaning.* New York, NY: Pocket Books, 1963.

Good, Timothy. *Above Top Secret.* New York, NY: William Marrow Co., 1988.

Graham, Billy. *Approaching Hoofbeats: The Four Horsemen of the Apocalypse.* Waco, TX: Word Books, 1983.

Gravel, Tara. "The Interview with David Jacobs, Ph.D.," Temple University Journalism Paper, December 6, 1990.

Gross, Martin L. *The Psychological Society.* New York, NY: Random House, 1978.

Hubbard, Barbara Mary. *The Revelation.* Novato, CA: Nataraj Publishing, 1995.

Ice, Thomas and Timothy Demy. *The Truth About the Last Days' Temple.* Eugene, OR: Harvest House, 1997.

Ingram, Chip. "What We Must Learn From the Killings at Columbine High." Living on the Edge, P.O. Box 2370, Santa Cruz, California, 1999 (Sermon).

International Christian Concern. "Global Persecution Update: Pakistan," August 9, 1998 (www.persecution.org).

International Christian Concern. October 22, 1998.

Shea, Nina. *In the Lion's Den: A Shocking Account of the Persecution and Martyrdom of Christians Today and How We Should Respond.* Nashville, TN: Broadman and Holman, 1997.

Kovel, Joel. *A Complete Guide to Therapy: From Psychoanalysis to Behavior Modification.* New York, NY: Pantheon Books, 1976.

LaHaye, Tim and Jerry Jenkins. *Are We Living in the End Times?* Wheaton, IL: Tyndale House Publishers, 1999.

Lalonde, Peter & Paul. *2000 A.D.* Nashville, TN: Thomas Nelson Inc., 1997.

Lewis, C. S. *Mere Christianity.* New York, NY: Macmillan, 1947.

Lindsey, Hal. *Apocalypse Code.* Palos Verdes, CA: Western Front Ltd., 1997.

Lindsey, Hal. *Planet Earth: The Final Chapter.* Beverly Hills, CA: Western Front Ltd., 1998.

Lindsey, Hal. *Satan Is Alive and Well on Planet Earth.* Grand Rapids, MI: Zondervan Publishing Company, 1972.

Mack, John. *Abductions.* New York, NY: Ballantine Books, 1994.

McDowell, Josh. *Evidence That Demands a Verdict.* San Bernardino, CA: Here's Life Publishers, 1979.

Meldau, Fred John. *Messiah in Both Testaments.* Denver, CO: The Christian Victory Publishing Company, 1956.

Minirth, Frank and Paul Meier. *Counseling and the Nature of Man.* Grand Rapids, MI: Baker Book House, 1982.

Missler, Chuck and Mark Eastman. *Alien Encounters.* Coeur d'Alene, ID: Koinonia House, 1997.

Montgomery, Ruth. *Ruth Montgomery: Herald of the New Age.* New York, NY: Doubleday, 1986.

Morris, Desmond. *The Naked Ape.* New York, NY: McGraw Hill, 1969.

Nature, Vol. 294: 105, November 12, 1981.

Pentecost, J. Dwight. *Things to Come.* Grand Rapids, MI: Zondervan Publishing House, 1974.

Plain Dealer Newspaper, Cleveland, Ohio, March 31, 1996, 1F, Plain Dealer Publishing Company.

Redfield, James. *The Celestine Prophecy.* New York, NY: Warner Books, 1993.

Ross, Hugh. *Beyond the Cosmos.* Colorado Springs, CO: Nav Press, 1999.

Sakoloff, Boris. *The Permissive Society.* New Rochelle, NY: Arlington House, 1971.

Schaeffer, Francis A. *The God Who Is There.* Downers Grove, IL: InterVarsity Press, 1968.

Simmons, Christine. *Prophecy.* Dallas, TX: Southwestern Typographics, 1978.

Stranges, Frank F. *Stranger at the Pentagon*. New Brunswick, NJ: Inner Light Publications, 1991.

Thomas, I.D.E. *The Omega Conspiracy*. Oklahoma City, OK: Hearthstone Publishing, 1986.

Time Magazine. September 30, 1971.

Time Magazine. December 6, 1999, p.1 (Agilent Technologies - Innovating the HP Way).

UFO Universe (September 1998).

Vallee, Jacques. *Dimensions*. New York, NY: Ballantine Books, 1988.

Walvoord, John F. and Roy B. Zuck. *The Bible Knowledge Commentary, Old Testament*. Wheaton, IL: Victor Books, Scripture Publications, 1985.

Walvoord, John F. and Roy B. Zuck. *The Bible Knowledge Commentary, New Testament*. Wheaton, IL: Victor Books, Scripture Publications, 1983.

Walvoord, John F. *Major Bible Prophecies*. Grand Rapids, MI: Zondervan Publishing House, 1991.

Walvoord, John F. *The Revelation of Jesus Christ*. Chicago, IL: Moody Press, 1966.